MW01268863

Harmony Hall – Battersee

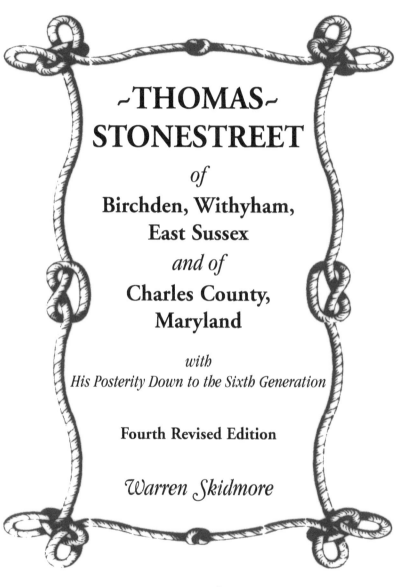

~THOMAS~
STONESTREET

of

**Birchden, Withyham,
East Sussex**

and of

**Charles County,
Maryland**

with
His Posterity Down to the Sixth Generation

Fourth Revised Edition

Warren Skidmore

HERITAGE BOOKS
2012

HERITAGE BOOKS

AN IMPRINT OF HERITAGE BOOKS, INC.

Books, CDs, and more—Worldwide

For our listing of thousands of titles see our website
at
www.HeritageBooks.com

Published 2012 by
HERITAGE BOOKS, INC.
Publishing Division
100 Railroad Ave. #104
Westminster, Maryland 21157

Other Heritage Books by the author:

*Basil Williams of South Wales, and Seneca Hundred, Montgomery County, Maryland by 1748,
with Some Notes on His Distinquished Kinfolk in Pennsylvania, Virginia, Kentucky and Elsewhere*

*Lord Dunmore's Little War of 1774: His Captains and Their Men
Who Opened Up Kentucky and the West to American Settlement*
Warren Skidmore with Donna Kaminsky

*Thomas Stonestreet of Birchden, Withyham, East Sussex, and of Charles County, Maryland,
with His Posterity Down to the Sixth Generation
Fourth Revised Edition*

International Standard Book Numbers
Paperbound: 978-0-7884-1694-1
Clothbound: 978-0-7884-9480-2

CONTENTS

INTRODUCTION

The Stonestreets of Maryland are (from the viewpoint of the family historian) a delight. They were not much given to wearing down their wives with   enormous families, and they still survive in tidy and manageable numbers. For the most part they were born (from the second generation onward) to be prosperous tobacco planters which was, short of the learned professions, the appropriate calling for a country gentleman in lower Maryland. Harry Wright Newman, a diligent genealogist of the place and period (and himself doubly descended from the Stonestreets) lumps them with the families he considered Charles County gentry.

The Stonestreets had some laudable virtues. The Charles County planter might have nicotine-stained fingers and calluses but he had a high regard for education. Several of them were teachers and the Reverend Charles H. Stonestreet, S.J., went on to become an early president of Georgetown University in Washington, D.C. Several members of the family, the present writer included, were students at St. John's College at Annapolis.

The family was as a whole reasonably affluent and consequently generally given to probate. Their deeds and wills survive in generous numbers, but this is not to say that there are not some riddles left for others to solve. An initial complication was the large number of Stonestreet men with the otherwise uncommon given name *Butler*. They had their name from Elizabeth Butler, the wife of the first Thomas Stonestreet in Maryland. Happily all these men named Butler eventually sorted themselves out satisfactorily.

The name Stonestreet is from the paved Roman road called *Stanistreet* that ran in ancient times from London to Chicester in Sussex. The surname is found in the medieval period almost always along the road in Sussex, but by the time of the Tudors the family had spread to Kent and London and occasionally elsewhere. Although the name has always been rare in England it seems likely that more than one man took his name from his residence and that Stonestreet is not necessarily Stonestreet's cousin everywhere.

The family at Birchden in Sussex is quite obscure and we have not found any probates, chancery suits, or court records for them. At the moment all we have are the extracts from the Bishop's transcripts for Withyham parish which replaces in large part the register lost when the church was struck by lightning and was totally destroyed on 16 June 1663. They are printed here in Appendix I.

It should be noted here that the Stonestreets of Maryland have no right to use the coat-of-arms (*Argent on two bars sable 3 bulls' heads, caboshed, argent between two wings, elevated sable*). Nothing that I printed in earlier editions of this book provoked as much invective from the family as this statement! The fact is that this coat was granted by the College of Heralds in London to a Stonestreet family who were mercers at Hailsham, Sussex. They were *not* ancestors to the Charles County family, although they were probably cousins in some unknown way. My grandmother had a framed copy of the bulls' heads on her parlor wall, probably a gift from her uncle Charles Edward Stonestreet (1844-1917) who was very much interested in his family's history. It seems to have circulated widely among several branches of the family in America in the Victorian period. These copies may have come from Doctor Ancus M. Hoffar of Washington, D.C., who did a fair amount of research on the family. He was seemingly wrongly convinced that his Stonestreet wife was entitled to some unclaimed family fortune in England.

v

A great many people have had a hand in the making of this book. Two of them need to be singled out for special appreciation. Claire (Mrs. Glen W.) Hubbard of Carmichael, California, did much of the research and turned up many of the evidences cited hereafter. She might very well appear as a joint author, but this would saddle her with a part of the blame for my errors and other insufficiencies. The late Guy W. Stonestreet, also educated at St. John's, scoured the Charles County countryside in pursuit of his family and their houses and contributed much of what is printed here about Colonel Nicholas Stonestreet and La Grange, standing still, his ancestral home.

In the fifth edition of this book I assumed that Butler Stonestreet (no. 3) lived at the house now called Harmony Hall, which was built on the old plantation called Battersea in Prince George's County. Since the publication of the last edition of this book the evidences for the descent of Harmony Hall has been thoroughly checked separately by myself and by a formal historian of the property appointed by the National Park Service. It now appears certain that Butler Stonestreet probably did own by 1747 all of the 500 acres that formerly made up Battersea. Alas, some deeds to him as a grantee for Battersea are clearly missing, and more importantly a good many deeds from his heirs as grantors disposing of parts of Battersea after his death were never recorded by the purchasers. Some bits of evidence were overlooked in the Park Service study, who came to the conclusion that Harmony Hall probably descended from some unknown heir or devisee of the Tyler family to Enoch Magruder. I see no firm evidence for this, although I concur that the earliest *proven* owner of Harmony Hall was probably James Marshall, a merchant, who did sell 100 acres of Battersea to Enoch Magruder on the 6 September 1769. After a close look at all of the evidence I believe that the house was built on land probably formerly owned by the Tylers, but which they must have sold by 1733 to Thomas Stonestreet who worked very hard to reassemble the moieties of old Battersea. If Stonestreet did not build the house he appears to have owned it three years later in 1726, and certain quitclaim deeds show that it must have been his by 1747. However the title to the *site* of Harmony Hall (but not the house) from the Tylers to the National Park Service remains cloudy. I have presented such evidences as survive elsewhere.

Warren Skidmore

FIRST GENERATION

1. THOMAS[1] STONESTREET, ancestor to the distinguished family of his name in Maryland, was born almost certainly at Birchden in Withyham, Sussex. He is probably the Thomas christened there as a son of Edward *Stonestrete* on 14 July 1630.[1] He died at Morris' Help, his plantation in Newport Hundred, Charles County, Maryland, in October (or November) 1706. He married Elizabeth Butler in Maryland, who died before him.

Thomas Stonestreet was brought into the province of Maryland at the expense, patronage and care of William Waters, a cousin of Captain Miles Cooke, a mariner. Waters wrote to Cooke on 3 February 1662/3:

> "Cousin Cook be pleased as soon as you have opportunity to enter the names of my four servants [Thomas Francis, Thomas Stonestreet, Thomas Miller, and George Shaw] in the Secretary's office for I must do it or else I may lose my land... for my grant is that I shall bring into the Province four servants yearly for five years. Pray, Cousin, be mindful of me in this, not else. I rest, your loving cousin and hum[ble] servant, William Waters."[2]

He had married his wife Elizabeth Butler by September 1688 when Thomas Stonestreet (a servant of William Barton) proved his right to 150 acres of land for himself, his wife Elizabeth Stonestreet (servant to James Walker), and the headright due to Edward Appleby who had transported himself to Maryland and had assigned his 50 acre right to Thomas Stonestreet. On 30 January 1668/9 he had a grant from Charles Calvert of a 150 acre plantation in what in now Charles County (but which was then reckoned as in St. Mary's County). The boundaries are given as:

> "beginning at a bound tree of Richard Morrices being a white oak, running eastward by south for length two hundred and ten perches to a bounded red oak, thence running southwest and by south for breadth two hundred and sixty perches to a bounded red oak joining to the land of Edward Swann, thence until it meets with the first bounded tree, containing and now laid out for one hundred and fifty acres, more or less"

which he called Birchden for his old home in England. For this he was to pay a rent of three shillings a year in equal portions at the two feasts of Annunciation or Lady Day (March 25th) and at Michaelmas (September 29th). One whole year's rent was to be paid each time the land was alienated.[3]

Thomas Stonestreet was a freeholder by 5 June 1668 when we find that "Thomas Stonestreet desires his marke of Cattle to be recorded (Vizt) a T on the Right ear and a cropp and an Underkeell on the Left."[4]

---

[1]Bishop's transcript of Withyham, Sussex, 1630. Copy at the Guildhall Library, London. See Appendix I at the end of this volume.

[2]Land Office, Annapolis, Maryland, liber 5, folio 221.

[3]Ibid., liber 12, folio 420-1.

[4]*Archives of Maryland*, volume 57, page 335. References to printed works have been cited in italics.

On 1 May 1672 Thomas Stonestreet and John Sheppard were granted letters patent to a plantation which they called Chessam. Sheppard had a right to 100 acres but he had assigned 50 of these to Stonestreet and they became joint proprietors. It adjoined a plantation called The Desert belonging to Robert Page. An annual rent of two shillings was to be paid for Chessam and the patent also notes that the income from any royal mines on the land was excluded from the rights granted to the new proprietors.[5]

He also acquired another plantation of 100 acres in Charles County called Morris' Help in some unknown way, most likely by a deed that he never saw recorded. Morris' Help became his home, at least near the end of his life, and was left in his will to his eldest son Edward Stonestreet. Edward lived there as well, but it was sold by Edward's son Butler Stonestreet on 5 August 1754 to Philip Barton Key.

Thomas Stonestreet was still reckoned as living in St. Mary's County in July 1683 when he served on several juries impaneled in that county.[6] At some point in this period the boundaries between St. Mary's and Charles Counties many have been adjusted, or perhaps Birchden was newly surveyed and found to fall in Charles County. When his son Thomas Stonestreet sold Birchden on 9 March 1713 the deed specifically noted that it was Charles County, but that it was formerly in St. Mary's County.[7] As early as 13 June 1682 Thomas Stonestreet came to court in Charles County (now presumably his abode) and presented a woman servant named Mary Stephens who the court adjudged to be 19 years of age.[8]

Morris' Help has not been precisely located but it was clearly between the two hamlets of Wicomico (in Charles County) and Budds Creek (in St. Mary's County) which lie two miles apart on Budds Creek Road (State Route 234). Trinity Church Road, in Newport Hundred, runs due north out of Wicomico and the Wicomico River is a short distance away on the south. In this period travel by water was much easier than by land, and it is likely that the Stonestreets ventured down the wide Wicomico to the Potomac and from there across into Virginia. Thomas Stonestreet, Junior, clearly found a wife with roots in old Virginia.

On 9 August 1689 Thomas Davis, a constable of Newport Hundred in Charles County, advised the court that "Thomas Stonestreet of this county hath a son named Thomas Stonestreet of age to pay levys and hee doth refuse to give in his name in ye list of taxables."[9] Thomas Stonestreet and his son were both summoned to the next court scheduled for September 13th. They do not seem to have appeared but John Bayne, High Sheriff of Charles County, reported that "ye said Stonestreet is sensible of his Errour and hee hath putt in his sons name in ye list of taxables."[10]

Thomas Stonestreet had a succession of servants who worked off the costs of their transportation to Maryland on his plantations. On 13 June 1699 James McCongh was presented to court and judged to be 21 years of age. James Mohoy was brought to court on 13 March 1704/5 by Thomas Stonestreet, Senior, who swore under oath that Mohoy had been absent from his plantation for nine days. The court decreed that the "servant to serve his master ninety days after the expiration of his time of servitude."[11] On 31

---

[5]Land Office, liber 14, folio 484.
[6]*Archives of Maryland,* volume 50, pages 656, 660, 681, 707, 721, 730-1, 733- 4.
[7]Charles County Deeds, book D2, page 84.
[8]Ibid., book J, page 293.
[9]Ibid., book V, page 407.
[10]Ibid., book V, page 413.
[11]Ibid., book B2, book 61.

March 1705 Mary Rodd of Charles County, a spinster, bound her daughter of the same name (who was aged three on the 27th of September last) to Thomas Stonestreet, a planter of Charles County, to serve according to "ye Custom of the County in Such Cases."[12]

On 11 June 1706 Thomas Stonestreet conveyed by deed of gift the plantation known as Birchden to his son Thomas Stonestreet of Prince George's County "for & in consideration of natural love & affection which he hath & beareth toward the said Thomas, his son."[13] Thomas Stonestreet, the elder, died a few months later.

His wife Elizabeth was probably dead by this date. She was presumably the Elizabeth Butler who provided a headright for Humphrey Warren who lived on the Wicomico River in 1662. Both of her sons named sons Butler Stonestreet in her honor, and Butler as a Christian name persisted in several branches of this family as a given name for a number of generations. She died before her husband. The marriage was clearly harmonious as Thomas Stonestreet asked in his will to be buried "by or near my dear wife" probably (as was usual) somewhere at Morris' Help.

Thomas Stonestreet was alive on 14 October 1706 when he signed a relatively uncomplicated will "being very sick and weak of body." He left "my now dwelling plantation thereunto belonging called by the name of Morrises Helpe containing 100 acres of land" to his son Edward and his heirs lawfully begotten. He also left fifty acres to his grandson Butler (son of his son Thomas Stonestreet). To his grandson (and namesake) Thomas Mastin he left a cow and a calf with their increase. All of his personal estate was to be divided into four equal parts and his four children were each to have a share after his debts were paid.[14] The will notes, curiously, that two lines had been scraped out of it before it was sealed and signed.

His personal estate (land aside) was appraised at £86 17sh 7d in an inventory filed by his son Edward, the executor, on 11 January 1706/7. The inventory (which survives) lists largely items usually found in the households of the time, except for a looking glass which was accounted a luxury in the period.[15] An account was filed with court on 1 October 1707 and it lists an expense of 800 pounds of tobacco which had been paid for the funeral charges.[16] The early accounts of the estate gives the names of the two sons-in-law of Thomas Stonestreet which his will did not. They were Robert Hager and _____ Tedman.[17] Robert Hager is apparently the man of his name who died in 1710 in St. Mary's County, Maryland, leaving a wife Elizabeth and three children.[18] The final account of Hagar's estate was given 28 May 1715 and it shows that his widow Elizabeth had married Henry Nowell as her second husband by that date.[19] Of his Tedman son-in-law we know nothing except that his wife was formerly Sarah Stonestreet. He is likely to have been dead in 1707 since Sarah's legacy was paid directly to her and not (as was usual) to her husband.

---

[12]Ibid., book B2, page 127.
[13]Ibid., book C, page 7.
[14]Wills, Hall of Records (Annapolis), liber 12, folio 77.
[15]Inventories and Accounts, Hall of Records, liber 26, folio 189.
[16]Ibid., liber 27, folio 139.
[17]Inventories and Accounts, liber 28, folio 95 (18 December 1707). See also liber 32B, folio 258 (25 June 1711) where Sarah is called *Sedman* (an error in the printed abstract).
[18]*Maryland Calendar of Wills*, volume III, page 237.
[19]Inventories and Accounts, liber 36, folios 63-4.

The parents of his grandson Thomas Mastin also do not appear in the accounts. Presumably his mother was still alive in 1707 since the young Mastin (and his siblings, if any) would probably have been left an equal share of their mother's interest in Thomas Stonestreet's estate. If this is correct then presumably his mother (either Hager or Tedman) was previously the widow of Robert Mastin.[20]

        Children:

2.   i.   Edward, the eldest son, born about 1673.[21]
      ii.   Sarah, married _____ Tedman. She was probably already his widow in 1707.
     iii.   Elizabeth. She married firstly Robert Hager (died 1710), and secondly (by 1715) Henry Nowell of St. Mary's County, whom she survived.[22]
3.   iv.   Thomas, born about 1682.

---

[20]Robert Mastin was a witness on 16 January 1691/2 to the will of Joseph Pile. (*Maryland Calendar of Wills*, volume II, page 49.) Pile's plantation Sarum adjoined Stonestreet's Morris' Help. Thomas Stonestreet notes in his will of 14 October 1706 that he had leased 50 acres of Morris' Help to Joseph Pile [Junior] of Sarum.

[21]Debbie Hooper, *Abstracts of Chancery Court Records of Maryland 1669-1782*, 53. He testified on 20 April 1723 that he was about aged about 50.

[22]*Maryland Calendar of Wills*, volume VII, page 137. Henry Nowell's will is dated 28 November 1734 and was probated on 5 November 1735. He remembered his wife Elizabeth (presumably formerly Stonestreet), and his son Henry and a married daughter Frances Taylor (probably children of his first marriage). Robert Hager, doubtless a stepson, was a witness to Nowell's will.

SECOND GENERATION

2. EDWARD² STONESTREET of Morris' Help, son of Thomas (no. 1) and Elizabeth (Butler) Stonestreet, was born 1673 in Newport Hundred, Charles County, Maryland.[23] The name of his first wife is unknown, but she was probably the Thomasine (_____) Stonestreet who was with a certain Mary Slye called goddaughters by Michael Curtis in his will dated 13 July 1716. Thomasine Stonestreet was left a legacy of "one feather bed with one Rugg, one pair blanketts, two pair of sheets, one Doz'n of napkins, one Doz'n of pewter plates, two dishes, one Silver tumbler & one silver spoon." This was quite a handsome dowry for a young bride in the period. Mary Slye (who can not be fitted into the pedigree of the Slye family at present) was to have a silver tankard, a spoon and a breeding mare. It would be interesting to know their relationship to one another, if any, and to Curtis.[24]

Edward Stonestreet was married secondly (as a widower with several young children) to Susannah, a daughter of Robert and Priscilla (Goldsmith) Slye, Junior. She was previously the widow of Joseph Peters of St. Mary's County who had died in 1721. She was still Susannah Peters on 6 June 1722 when she swore that her first husband's inventory was just and perfect,[25] but on 5 March 1723 she and her new husband Edward Stonestreet turned in an accounting of the estate.[26] Edward Stonestreet died on 3 November 1749 at Morris' Help in Newport Hundred. He was buried from Trinity Church (three miles east of Wicomico, Maryland) close to his home.[27]

Edward Stonestreet had the parental homestead in 1706 under the terms of his father's will where he lived for the rest of his life. On 17 May 1714 Edward Stonestreet and George Whittier were bondsmen for John Compton, Senior, the administrator of his son John Compton, Junior, late of Charles County.[28] Stonestreet was granted letters of administration of the estate of Joshua Holdsworth, late of Charles County, on 18 January 1716/7 as the widow refused to serve. Francis Clark and George Whittier (once again) served as his bondsmen.[29]

Thomasine Stonestreet was apparently the mother of most of Edward's children. She may have been a Slye before her marriage and nearly related to his second wife Susannah. On 12 October 1753 John Slye, Butler Stonestreet's uncle, sold to him a part of the tract called Clear Doubt and the deed notes that it was "Part of the Same Land the said Butler and his [Slye] ancestors have for many years lived on."[30] Robert Slye,

---

[23]Debbie Hooper, *Abstracts of Chancery Court Records of Maryland, 1669-1782*, page 53.

[24]For a complete text of the will of Michael Curtis and a long discussion of the relationship of the legatees to Curtis, one another, and the Slye family, see the article by John Walton "The will of Michael Curtis" in the *National Genealogical Society Quarterly*, volume 58 (June 1970), 108-116.

[25]Inventories, Hall of Records, liber 7, folios 224-6.

[26]Accounts, Hall of Records, liber 25, folios 33-4.

[27]Trinity Church Register, page 183.

[28]Testamentary Proceedings, Hall of Records, liber 22, folio 352

[29]Ibid., liber 23, folio 85.

[30]Charles County Deeds, book A, page 146.

Senior (died 1670), of St. Clement's manor, had owned Clear Doubt and Lapworth in Charles County, and had been baptized 8 July 1627 at *Lapworth,* Warwickshire, the son of George Slye.[31] He emigrated to Maryland in 1654 bringing a number of retainers with him. He married Susannah Gerard and his lands went at his death in 1670 to his son Robert Slye II. The young Robert married Priscilla Goldsmith and left (in addition to his son John) three minor daughters named Judith, Susannah and Sarah at his death in 1698.[32] Susannah Slye married Edward Stonestreet and her son Butler (no. 5) and grandson Thomas (no. 10) both had financial dealings (noticed later) with Robert Slye III of Lapworth.[33]

Edward Stonestreet left a will dated 19 December 1740 when he was "sick and weake in body." However he obviously recovered from this illness, and the will was not proved until some nine years later on 9 December 1749 -- about five weeks after his death.[34] Susannah Stonestreet was living in 1740 and she had Morris' Help for the term of her life. After her death it was to go to his son Butler who is called "my *Eldest* and well beloved Son." The exact wording here is most important as it suggests that Edward had another son who was dead in 1740 and not remembered in his will. Whatever personal estate remained after the death of his wife was to be divided among his *three* surviving children Butler Stonestreet, Elizabeth Newman, and Anne Owing.

These provisions in his will are perfectly straight-forward. However he also provided for a Susannah Pye Stonestreet who was to have 500 pounds of tobacco. Her relationship to Edward Stonestreet is left unstated. As the widow Susannah Pye Stonestreet she married secondly William Goodrum at Trinity Church on 20 December 1748.[35] That she was born a Pye (and *not* a Stonestreet) is made clear in the record of the christening of her children by Goodrum at Trinity Church where she is called Susannah *Pye.*[36] At the moment the evidence suggests that she was the widow (by 1740) of another son of Edward Stonestreet whose given name is not certainly known to us. In the Land Records of Prince George's County there is a long set of testimonies recorded on 28 June 1732 about the boundaries of a tract called Stony Harbor. One of those testifying was a *Pouth. Stonestreet,* a highly unlikely name, according to an abstract made by Elise Greenup Jourdan.[37] Nothing else is known of this man, but he may have been the husband of Susannah Pye.

---

[31]Lapworth is another splendid example of how a plantation name can suggest the origin of an American family beyond any doubt. Robert Slye swore in open court on 25 September 1661 that he was aged 34 or thereabouts which agrees perfectly with the Lapworth register.

[32]*Maryland Calendar of Wills,* I, 59, and II, 167.

[33]John Slye (the brother of Susannah Stonestreet) and his wife Eleanor Compton, were the parents of Robert III who was born on 15 November 1745 according to the register of Trinity Church. Eleanor (Compton) Slye was a daughter of John Compton, Senior, noticed earlier.

[34]Testamentary Proceedings, liber 33, folio 106. The witnesses were Thomas Ching, John Ching, and Joseph McCormick.

[35]Trinity Church Register, page 185.

[36]Ibid., pages 185, 188.

[37]Elise Greenup Jourdan, *The Land Records of Prince George's County, Maryland, 1726-1733,* page 172. The complete series of depositions will be found in Prince George's County Deeds, Book Q, pages 478-486, which has not been seen. *Pouth* may have been the Peter Stonestreet, also not identified, who was a petitioner in 1742 (with Edward and Thomas Stonestreet) to the governor and assembling asking that Prince George's County be divided.

The Pye family does not seem to have attracted a historian in Maryland. In England the Reverend Charles J. Robinson wrote an excellent account of the Pyes of the Mynde in Much Dewchurch, Herefordshire, published in 1873.[38] The Pyes were prominent at Court, and his tabular pedigree of the British family includes Edward Pye (who married Ann, daughter of Nicholas Snell, Secretary to Lord Baltimore, and widow of Benjamin Rozier of the *Potohomock* [*sic*] River, Maryland). Their son Walter Pye, married "_____, daughter of John Faunt of St. Mary's, co. Maryland." To this we can add that Walter's wife was *Margaret*, daughter of John *Tant* or *Taunt*. Robinson also states that this Walter died without issue, but this is not the case. Margaret, the widow of John Tant, in her will names her *daughter* Margaret Pye and her *grandson* Walter Pye.[39] Alas, this is the only probate record that we have mentioning the Pyes in the young Walter II's generation. From deeds we know that he had a brother Charles, and (by elimination) it would appear at least two sisters Susanna and Margaret Pye both of whom married first cousins named Stonestreet. Margaret Pye (noticed later) married Edward Stonestreet (no. 7) about 1728 as his first wife.[40] Finally, it must be mentioned that Susanna Pye's children by her Stonestreet husband, if any, disappear from view.

    Children: (by his first wife)

4.   i.   Thomas, eldest son.
     ii.   [Perhaps a younger son, married Susannah Pye as her first husband?]
     iii. Elizabeth, married (by 1730) William Newman, Junior, of Charles County. [Their son, Butler Newman, married Verlinda Stonestreet to be noticed later.]
     iv.   Ann, married (by 1737) Richard Owings III (1711-1790). They moved in 1757 to the south side of the Wateree River in what is now Laurens County, South Carolina.[41]

                   (by his second wife)

5.   v.   Butler.

3. THOMAS[2] STONESTREET of Battersea, the second son of Thomas (no. 1) and Elizabeth (Butler) Stonestreet, was born about 1682 in Newport Hundred, Charles County.[42] He married late in 1702 Christian, the widow of William Coghill of Port Tobacco in Charles County. Her family name has not been discovered in Maryland, but she may very well have been a daughter of some unknown family across the Potomac in Old Rappahannock County, Virginia. Thomas Stonestreet died, a widower, in September 1771

---

[38]Charles J. Robinson, *A History of the Mansions and Manors of Herefordshire* (London, 1873), 85-8.
[39]*Maryland Calendar of Wills*, V, 200.
[40]Walter Pye II died intestate, and his son Edward married Sarah Edelen (previously the widow of Samuel Queen), on 24 February 1735 at St. John's, Piscataway. They were the grandparents of Mary Olivia Pye who married Colonel Nicholas Stonestreet (no. 30) to be noticed later. Sarah Edelen was born 19 February 1705, the daughter of Edward and Elizabeth (Jenkins) Edelen.
[41]For her posterity see *Owings and allied families, a genealogy of some of the descendants of Richard Owings I of Maryland 1685-1975*, by Addison D. Owings (1975).
[42]Prince George's County Deeds, book Q, page 297, and book Y, page 236. He stated that he was aged about 49 in 1731, and about 57 in 1740.

at Battersea in Upper Piscataway Hundred, Prince George's County, Maryland.

William Coghill, the first husband of Christian Stonestreet, was a son of the James Coghill of Old Rappahanock County, Virginia, whose will was proved on 2 September 1685. William Coghill and his unnamed wife executed a deed on 26 March 1689 in Charles County for lands in Rappahanock County (but recorded in Essex County, Virginia). William Coghill died in August 1702.[43] His wife, left in comfortable circumstances with three young sons, wasted (as usual) no time in finding a second husband. Things were difficult indeed for a young widow who had farms and livestock, as well as slaves, to manage without a man about the plantation.

We have already noticed that Thomas Stonestreet had Birchden as a gift from his father on 11 June 1706, when he was already identified as being of Prince George's County. On 9 March 1713/4, called a planter, he sold the whole of Birchden (150 acres) to Thomas Lewis of Charles County, for 5000 pounds of tobacco.[44]

Thomas Stonestreet had moved by 1703 to Piscataway Hundred which fell into Prince George's County when it was formed in 1695. What occasioned his removal is unknown, but it may have been his marriage to the widow Coghill. He set about acquiring a great plantation of 500 acres called Battersea by determined degrees. A study of the titles to the various parts of Battersea (which had earlier been sold off in different directions) is of some importance, for the fine brick manor house at Battersea now known as Harmony Hall is the oldest residence still standing in Prince George's County. Battersea had started out as 500 acres patented in 1662 by Humphrey Haggett, a young lawyer practicing before the Provincial Court. He never lived there, and divided the tract in 1688 selling half to Philip Mason and half to Richard Iles. Mason sold his half of 250 acres four years later to Thomas Lewis, Senior.

What decided Thomas Stonestreet to put the whole of old Battersea back together is unknown. His first purchase of 100 acres was made on 22 February 1709 from Thomas Lewis, Junior (who had Birchden from him soon after), and his brother Richard Lewis.[45] On 29 July 1709 Richard Lewis sold another 100 acres of the Mason moiety (including his parent's home built by 1692) to William Tyler, a carpenter.[46] Tyler apparently gave up carpentry as a trade, and turned the Lewis homestead into an ordinary to serve the local population. Harmony Hall has recently been the subject of an archaeological dig. The archaeologists

---

[43]*Maryland Calendar of Wills*, II, 252.

[44]Charles County Deeds, book C2, page 7, also Deeds D2, 84 at the Hall of Records, Annapolis. William Hickford Leman of Port Tobacco was appointed as their attorney to make the formal conveyance.

[45]Prince George's County Deeds, book E, page 5. Thomas Lewis, Junior, seems to have settled soon after at Birchden. He had died before 12 June 1739 when his three daughters Mary (wife of Joseph Hunt), Elizabeth (wife of Joseph Fry), and Ann (wife of William Robins) joined together to sell Birchden (150 acres) to Benjamin Thorn, a wheelright of Charles County. (Charles County Deeds, book O2, page 402). The title to Birchden has not been pursued beyond this date, but we will meet the Lewis family again in Loudoun County, Virginia.

[46]Ibid., book D, page 79. It is described as being northwest of the 100 acres already in the possession of William Tyler. The deed notes that this was a bequest of his father (whose will of 8 June 1696 stated that this included the house where Richard's mother Katherine Lewis then lived). Richard Lewis was presumably still unmarried. On 20 August 1707 his servant girl was cited to the Prince George's court for having produced a bastard child which she stated was fathered by Lewis.

concluded that the old Lewis house was destroyed by fire after 1715 but before 1720. Other evidences suggest that a new house, now Harmony Hall, was built nearby on the Tyler property in 1723.[47]

Thomas Stonestreet and Robert Butler were the two witnesses when Tyler willed the earlier *frame* house on the tract on 18 April 1718 to his wife Elizabeth, which was to go after her death to his son William, Junior. Tyler's last renewal of his license to run his ordinary was granted by the Prince George's Court in June 1721. Tyler was dead by 25 January 1722 when his will was proved by Stonestreet and Butler. On the same day Stonestreet and Christopher Edelen were securities in the sum of £500 for the widow to serve as executrix. Elizabeth Tyler was married soon after to Henry Massey, her second husband, and lived on until 1757.[48] What happened to the Tyler's 100 acres (had from Lewis and part of the original Battersea) at her second marriage is unknown. It seems likely (but unproven) that they were purchased by Thomas Stonestreet and it was he who built Harmony Hall there soon after in 1723. Tyler was dead by this date and his ordinary (burned, presumably to the ground) disappears from record. The Tylers had other lands elsewhere and there is nothing to suggest that William Tyler, Junior, ever lived at Battersea. In his will dated 24 January 1755 calls he calls himself "of Pomonkey."[49] He made very specific bequests to his three children but neither his will nor the will of his mother (who outlived him by two years) mention Battersea. We next hear of this part of the Battersea plantation in a deed for 100 acres from James Marshall to Enoch Magruder, a merchant, dated 6 September 1769. How Marshall came by this 100 acres -- which included Harmony Hall -- is unknown. It has been said (probably in error) that it came from either the Tyler heirs or their devisees. Marshall's deed refers to Magruder's dwelling nearby, probably at Want Water which adjoined Battersea on the east.[50]

One other deed survives to Thomas Stonestreet about the Lewis half of old Battersea plantation. On 20 August 1711 he had the last 50 acres of the Lewis moiety from John Lewis for 5000 pounds of tobacco. This half of Battersea (which is specifically stated to contain 250 acres) had been divided among the three heirs of Thomas Lewis, the elder, as directed by his will.[51] This final deed from John Lewis notes that his 50 acres bordered the part devised to his brother Thomas by their father Thomas Lewis, Senior, deceased, and it was already improved with buildings, dwellings, barns, outhouses, and orchards.

The descent of the other 250 acres of Battersea sold by Haggett to Richard Iles passed to Richard Gambra,

---

[47]The date of 1723 for the building of Harmony Hall can safely be tied to the construction of St. John's Church just up the road, from the same pinkish bricks fired at the same time and place. St. John's was built by a contractor named John Lane in 1723.

[48]Prince George's Accounts, book 5, page 17, gives on 7 February 1722 a list of the debts to be paid out of the estate of William Tyler by his wife Elizabeth and her second husband Henry Massey. The Masseys lived later (presumably immediately after their marriage) in what is now Sugarland Hundred, Montgomery County, Maryland. Massey's home was still in Prince George's (later Frederick, now Montgomery) County on 18 July 1747 when the inventory of his estate was taken (Prince George's Inventories, book 35, page 120). Elizabeth Massey's will is dated 15 March 1757, and left her estate to her surviving daughters (Prince George's Wills, book 30, page 243). She was dead by May 17th of the same year when an inventory of her estate was made. See also Harry Wright Newman, *Charles County Gentry* (Baltimore, 1971), 236-7.

[49]Charles County Wills, book 29, page 370.

[50]Prince George's County Deeds, book AA2, page 22.

[51]Ibid., book E, page 37.

Senior. On 15 November 1726 Thomas Stonestreet, planter, purchased from Richard Gambrill [sic], son and heir of Richard Gambra, late of Prince Georges County, the Gambra portion of Battersea "lying near Broad Creek *and adjoining the now dwelling-plantation of the said Thomas Stonestreet and Clash Creek.*" It seems likely that the dwelling-plantation mentioned in this deed was the house (now three years old) known as Harmony Hall. Clash Creek runs along the southern boundary of old Battersea, and adjoins the former Tyler lands at that place. The consideration for the Gambra purchase was 5000 pounds of tobacco plus £30 of English currency. On 17 January 1740 Thomas Stonestreet gave part of this tract "for love and natural affection" to his son Butler who was already living there. This tract consisted of 125 acres was described as "near Clash Creek and lying on the side of Fowkes Branch" together with all of the improvements that had been acquired from Gumbrill.[52] Two days later on 25 February 1740 he requested that a survey of Battersea be done by the Land Commission.[53]

Finally on 20 February 1747 and 26 May 1750 Thomas Stonestreet had quitclaim deeds from Samuel Mason and Thomas Thompson to protect his title to the whole 500 acres of Battersea. In both of these deeds two mythical 15 acres tracts were invented, one for the Lewis moiety and another 15 acres for the Gambra half. Samuel Mason's deed mentions his father Philip Mason's deed for 250 acres to Thomas Lewis dated 19 July 1692 "& it appears that there is about 15 acres still remaining of the original tract of Land called Batterzee." For a trifling £2 Mason gave Stonestreet a deed for this, but more importantly at the same time "relinquished any right of title to the Estate of Batterzee"-- the real business at hand.[54] Thompson signed a similiar quitclaim for £2 for his fictitious 15 acres and his interest in the Gambra moiety.[55] The big moment was now at hand, for Stonestreet clearly had reunited the original 500 acres of old Battersea and he and his son Butler had them in their possession. There remained to the father 275 acres of Battersea for which he remitted quit rents to the Lord Proprietory continuously from 1753 to 1772.[56]

The house and grounds (badly overgrown) of Harmony Hall were sold in 1966 by Mr. and Mrs. Charles W. Collins (who retained a life tenancy in the property) to the National Park Service. Harmony Hall remains a fine two and half story brick house, unspoiled by later additions, standing six miles south of the District of Columbia line on the west side of Livingston Road between the intersection of Old Fort and Fort Washington Roads.[57] Mrs. Collins survived until 1983 and the property was then let by the Park Service as a private residence and horse farm to lessors who were required to restore the buildings and grounds

---

[52]Thomas Stonestreet's deed of gift was recorded on 25 February 1740 in the Prince Georges County Deeds, book Y, page 256, on February 25th.

[53]Ibid., book BB1, page 327.

[54]Ibid., book EE, page 370, and book PP, page 49.

[55]Ibid., book PP, page 49. These two quitclaim deeds were unfortunately not abstracted at the time of the title search done for the National Park Service, nor did their "*Brief overview*" note that the Tylers and Masseys disappeared forever from Piscataway Hundred immediately after the death of William Tyler, Senior. The fictitious nature of these two quit claim deeds should be compared to the Feet of Fines which at this date was the chief method of conveying a freehold estate in England. In these a fictitious dispute between a purchaser (the querient) and the seller (the deforciant) was recorded, wherein for the return of a specified sum the seller quit any future claim which he or his heirs might have to the land either for an agreed period or forever. Fines were not abolished in England until 1834.

[56]Debt Books, Land Office, Annapolis.

[57]American Guide Series, *Maryland, a new guide to the old line state* (1976), page 289.

to the agency's specifications. An archeologist and historian were appointed to advise the lessors and the Park Service authorized the start of archaeological field work about Harmony Hall.[58]

Thomas Stonestreet was also a large slave owner. The earliest bill of sale found of his slaves is dated 4 August 1733 when James Ranton sold Thomas Stonestreet a negro boy named Jack and a negro girl called Kate for £30 sterling.[59] On 14 May 1768 Thomas Stonestreet, planter, signed an instrument providing that "in and for consideration of the faithful service & Labor of my mulatto woman Patience [she is] to have her absolute & full freedom after my decease."[60]

A few early tax lists survive for Piscataway Hundred in Prince George's County, and in 1719 Thomas Stonestreet and his stepson William Coghill are found as neighbors there.[61] In 1733 Thomas and his sons Butler and Edward Stonestreet are among the taxables in Upper Piscataway, while Thomas was the Constable charged with collecting the tax in Lower Piscataway Hundred.[62]

The *American Weekly Mercury* published at Philadelphia on 11 October 1733 had an advertisement placed by Thomas Stonestreet for John Spaw, his convict servant and a butcher by trade, who was a runaway.

Thomas Stonestreet and his family were members of St. John's (or Piscataway) Church in Piscataway Hundred founded in 1692.[63] It was less than a mile from Battersea. The present church, built in 1723 as noticed earlier, is a rectangular pinkish brick building. It was the third edifice on the site. The first mention of the Stonestreets in the register appears on 26 August 1703 when the birth of Butler, the son of Thomas and Christian Stonestreet, was recorded.

Thomas Stonestreet's death was noticed in the *Maryland Gazette* published at Annapolis on 12 September 1771: "Last week in Prince George's County Thomas Stonestreet, a native of that county, aged beyond all doubt ninety eight, but more probably appears from circumstances 105 or 106." Thomas Stonestreet was probably about 89 at the time of his death. He was not as old as 105, nor was he born in Prince George's County (although he may very well have been its oldest resident).

His will is dated 2 April 1771. He had given a part of Battersea to his son Butler Stonestreet, who died

---

[58]*Washington Post*, 12 August 1985. Two useful documents were produced by the appointees: "*Brief overview of [the] History of Occupation of Battersea and Want Water (Harmony Hall) Prince Georges County, Maryland,*" by Marilyn W. Nickels and Barbara Grady, was submitted to the National Parks Service on 12 December 1986. It collected most, but not all, of the early references to Battersea in the Prince George's County records. I have added a good many other references taken from the microfilms of the county records at the Family History Library at Salt Lakle City. Also a paper "*The Late Seventeenth Century Western Frontier of Maryland: A View From Harmony Hall*" by Stephen R. Potter, Ph.D. and Robert C. Sonderman, was presented at a session of the Society for Historical Archaeology held at Baltimore on 7 January 1989. I am greatly indebted to Lois Evans Holliday of Ashton, Maryland, for copies of both, as well as several photographs of the house.
[59]Prince Georges County Deeds, book Q, page 680.
[60]Prince George's County Deeds, book BB2, page 255.
[61]Calendar of Maryland State Papers, *No. 1 The Black Books* (1967), page 24, ref. 164.
[62]Ibid., page 40, ref. 268.
[63]The vestry proceedings begin in 1693, and the parish register in 1701.

before his father, on 23 February 1740. This tract of 175 acres had been purchased from Richard Gambrill as that deed of gift clearly states.[64] Some part of what remained of Battersea he gave to his surviving son Edward Stonestreet in his will. No acreage is mentioned in the will, but it must have been part the 275 acres on which he had paid a quit rent to the Proprietor. By elimination it would appear that Edward Stonestreet had as his share the part of Battersea purchased from the Lewis heirs, with perhaps an addition. Edward's part was to begin "at a gum tree that stands on the right hand of the path that goes from my dwelling-plantation house to Butler Newman's house [his grandson by marriage] where he now lives … then down the branch that connects with his spring … until it intersects a parcel of land which I gave to my son Butler Stonestreet out of Battacy [sic]."

The remainder of Battersea (unfortunately no acreage or description is given) was to be divided between his four grandsons John, Basil, Butler, and Edward Stonestreet.[65] In addition to their bequests of land John Stonestreet was to have a negro man called Charles; Basil a negro man called Ed; Edward a negro boy called Harry; and Butler a negro man called Massey. Verlinda, his granddaughter and the wife of Butler Newman, was to have a negro girl named Betsy and a negro woman called Cate. His granddaughter Verlinda Lanham was to have a feather bed and blanket. His daughter Anne Lowe was given a shilling "and no more Besides what I gave her in my Life Time which I thought sufficient." Elizabeth Ashford, another daughter, was to have £4 in addition to what her father had given her earlier. Patience was again confirmed in her freedom "and to be at her Liberty free or Clare from any servitude from any person whatsoever." His negro Jack was to be sold to the best advantage and the money divided among his son Edward and his four grandsons. His four grandsons were to have all his personal property equally, except any ready cash which his son Edward was to have. Edward and his grandson John were appointed executors. An inventory of his estate was taken of 18 December 1771 by Robert Wade, Senior, and Edward Clarkson. It totaled £565 5sh 6d and was approved by Basil W. Stonestreet and Edward Stonestreet as the next of kin. With much more it included a pewter tankard, 11 negro slaves, and wearing apparel worth £4.[66] The will was proved on 28 November 1771.[67]

Children: (all christened at St. Johns Church at Piscataway)

6.   i.   Butler, born 26 August 1703.
7.   ii.   Edward born 23 December 1705.
     iii.   Thomas, born 7 June 1708. He probably died young.
     iv.   Anne, born 23 March 1710/1 She married John Hawkins Lowe (1716-1792) and they were both living in 1776 in St. John's parish.[68]

---

[64]Prince George's County Deeds, book Y, page 256.

[65]On 13 June 1780 John Stonestreet purchased the interest of his brother Butler in Battersea which had descended to them from their grandfather Thomas Stonestreet. (Prince George's County Deeds, book FI-1, page 41.) He paid Butler Stonestreet £275 for his undivided quarter part of Battersea so it would seem that this part of the plantation must have been reckoned as worth about of £1100. Presumably he also acquired the interest of his brothers Basil and Edward but these deeds unfortunately are not on record in the county. There is yet a final mystery: no record has been found of what happened to John Stonestreet's interest (partial or complete) for this segment of Battersea!

[66]The original inventory will be found in Box 23, folder 16, at the Hall of Records.

[67]Will book 38, page 465.

[68]*Maryland Records*, ed. Gaius Marcus Brumbaugh, vol. I, page 74.

v.   Elizabeth, born 6 June 1714. She married John Ashford. He died in 1765 in Fairfax County, Virginia. She was remembered in her fathers will in 1771 but was dead before 20 November 1775 when her son sold land in Fairfax County.[69]

---

[69]Fairfax County, Virginia, Deeds, book M, page 163. On 30 January 1760 John and Elizabeth (Stonestreet) Ashford sold land in Fairfax County to [President] George Washington (Fairfax Deeds, book D, pages 823-5.) They had, with other children, a son Butler Stonestreet Ashford.

THIRD GENERATION

4. THOMAS³ STONESTREET was born about 1710-5 in Newport Hundred, Charles County, the son of Edward (no. 2) and Thomasine (_____) Stonestreet. He married Mary _____ who married John Farrand on 2 May 1743 at Trinity Church as her second husband.[70] John Farrand died testate in 1774 in Charles County survived by six children and his widow Mary.[71]

This Thomas must be distinguished from his cousin of the same name (born 7 June 1708), the son of his uncle Thomas Stonestreet (no. 3). The identification is certain since he named his only known child Thomasine for his mother. The Thomas born in 1708 disappears, and probably died young.

The birth of his daughter Thomasine was entered in the Trinity Church Register at the same time as her two eldest Farrand siblings.

      Child:

    i.   Thomasine, born 2 June 1741. She was living in 1749 but probably died young.

5. BUTLER³ STONESTREET of Morris' Help in East Newport Hundred, Charles County, was the only surviving son of Edward (no. 2) and Susannah (Slye) Stonestreet. He married Elizabeth, the daughter of James and Elizabeth (Shaw) Freeman of Piccowaxen Neck, who survived him. Butler Stonestreet died in 1774 between May 15th (when his will was signed) and July 28th (when it was proved).

On 12 October 1753 Butler Stonestreet of Charles County purchased 80 acres of a plantation called Clear Doubt from his uncle John Slye for 12,000 pounds of tobacco. It was between Gilbert Swamp and Bird Creek and the deed notes that "it being Part of the Same Land the said Butler and his ancestors have for many years lived on." John Slye's wife Eleanor surrendered her dower on the same day and on 20 November 1753 Butler Stonestreet paid 1sh 7d as an alienation fine.[72] Three days later he sold the same 80 acres to Philip Barton Key of St. Mary's County, and Elizabeth Stonestreet surrendered her right of dower.[73] On 7 October 1754 Butler Stonestreet sold Morris' Help to the same Philip Barton Key for 15,000 pounds of an inspected tobacco crop.[74] He was now landless, although he continues to be called a tobacco planter in the records.

Butler Stonestreet died in 1774. His will was dated on 15 May when he was "infirm of body." It was a relatively simple document; his wife was to be executrix and she was to have all his personal property

---

[70]Trinity Church Register, page 181.
[71]Ibid., page 193.
[72]Charles County Deeds, book A, page 141.
[73]Ibid., book A, page 146.
[74]Ibid., book A, page 233.

(horses, cattle, hogs, sheep, household furnishings, corn, and tobacco). At her death what remained was to be divided among his six children (who are named). Elizabeth offered the will for probate on 28 July 1774 in Charles County.[75]

His widow survived him by only a few months, and was dead by 20 April 1775. On 2 February 1776 Butler Stonestreet, her son and administrator, exhibited an inventory totaling £94 10sh 1/4d. This included her personal property, a crop of tobacco worth £20 16sh 2d, cash in her home, and a debt paid by Mathew Blair. Among the debts that Butler Stonestreet had paid were her doctor bills to Dr. Joseph Adderton, a year's rent of £10 on land leased from Daniel Heath, and the care of a crop of tobacco in a warehouse. Robert Slye and Thomas Givens were sureties for Butler Stonestreet. Her representatives (and heirs) were her six children.[76] Her next of kin are given most curiously as Nathan and *Mical* Freeman.

At the census of 1775 taken for Charles County only Butler Stonestreet and his brother Edward are enumerated living in East Newport Hundred.[77] Their younger brothers Thomas and James Freeman Stonestreet are not found. They did not subscribe to the Oath of Allegiance in Charles County during 1778 as proscribed by the State Legislature, but since both Butler and Edward both served in the Revolutionary Army it does appear that the family was of a proper Whiggish disposition.

Birth records for a part of his children are found at Trinity Church in Charles County.

Children:

8.	i.	Butler, born 20 October 1748.
9.	ii.	Edward, born 6 January 1754.
	iii.	Elizabeth, born 22 March 1757. She married _____ Mattingly and was living in 1785.
10.	iv.	Thomas.
	v.	Mary, born 22 March 1763. She married _____ Swann and was living in 1786.
11.	vi.	James Freeman.

6. **BUTLER³ STONESTREET** of Battersea was born 26 August 1703 in Piscataway Hundred, Prince George's County, the son of Thomas (no. 3) and Christian (_____) Stonestreet. He was twice married; firstly about 1733 to Frances, the daughter of Francis and Ann (Lowe) Tolson, and secondly to Jane (born 1718), the daughter of Christopher and Jane (Jones) Edelen.[78] Tolson was born at Wood Hall at Brightchurch, Cumberland, England, the son of Henry Tolson, Esq., on 22 September 1707. Stonestreet's widow Jane married secondly Clement Wheeler on 25 February 1759. She may have been dead by 22 September 1770 as she is not remembered in the will of her father signed on that day. Richard Edelen, the emigrant ancestor of her family died in 1694 in St. Marys County. He was from Pinner, Middlesex, the son of Reverend Philip Edelen buried in St. Mary's Church, Denham, Buckinghamshire, where there is a memorial to him on the south wall of the church. The Edelens were anciently from Hertfordshire. Butler

---

[75]Wills, book 6, page 199.
[76]Accounts, Hall of Records, liber 73, folio 369.
[77]*Maryland Records,* ed. G. M. Brumbaugh, I, 302.
[78]For the Tolson marriage see the *Maryland Genealogical Society Bulletin,* vol. 20, no. 2 (Spring 1979) 124, and for the Edelen family see Harry Wright Newman's *Charles County Gentry.*

Stonestreet died at Battersea in December 1755, and was doubtless buried from St. John's Church at Piscataway where his children were christened.

He married Frances Tolson soon after 21 December 1732; she was still unmarried on this date as the papers filed in the probate of her father show.[79] They were married by 26 February 1733/4 when an additional accounting of the estate of Francis Tolson show that Frances, his daughter, and her husband Butler Stonestreet were now acting as his administrators.[80] Frances Stonestreet had a share of her fathers land and personalty and was dead by 1743.

Butler Stonestreet acquired considerable land in Prince Georges County. He purchased a part of Wade's Adventure on 30 May 1738 from Richard Wade, Junior, for £46. It contained 115 acres on Horse Pond and Horse Pond Run, and was devised in his will to his posthumous son Butler Edelen Stonestreet.[81]

On 23 February 1740 he had 175 acres of Battersea as a gift from his parents Thomas and Christian Stonestreet.[82] He continued to live there until his death in 1755 when it passed to his son Richard Stonestreet.

He purchased a part of Littleworth, a plantation of 92 acres, from Isaac Cecil of Westmoreland County, Virginia, on 20 October 1747.[83] It also was devised to Richard Stonestreet in 1755.

A part of Exeter was purchased on 22 October 1748 from Edward Digges for £175 sterling.[84] It contained 216 acres and went to his eldest son Henry Stonestreet at his death.

Butler Stonestreet died in December 1755. His will was signed on the 3rd and proved on the 29th of the month. His lands were divided among his two sons, with the provision "that if the child wherewith my wife is now pregnant shall be a male child that he should have and enjoy the said tract of land [Wade's Adventure]." Butler Edelen Stonestreet, a son, was born two months after his fathers death and Wade's Adventure did indeed pass to him.

His two eldest sons were to have slaves (who are named) and his daughters had either slaves or gifts of tobacco (the ready money crop). His daughter Charity had a negro boy named Little Macy and a girl Henny. But his will notes that "whereas my daughter Charity is at this [time] dangerously ill, my will is that in case of her death the Negro boy named Little Macy and the negro girl named Henny shall belong to my daughter Mary Stonestreet."

He also provides that my "further will and earnest desire is that my sons be carefully educated in the principles of the Church of England as by law established." His friends John Tolson [formerly his brother-in-law], Luke Marbury and Henry Low were named as trustees and his wife Jane was to be the

[79]*Accounts*, Hall of Records, book 11, pages 567, 570-6.
[80]Ibid., book 12, page 212.
[81]Prince George's County Deeds, book T, page 586.
[82]Ibid., book Y, page 256.
[83]Ibid., book EE, page 321.
[84]Ibid., book EE, page 544.

executrix.[85] Some indication of the size of the estate is given by the amount of the bond required of the widow; on 8 April 1756 she posted a bond for £1500 with Christopher Edelen and John Edelen as her securities.

The inventory of his personal estate was taken on 17 May 1756. It totaled £195 15sh 2d and included 21 negroes, as well as one white servant who still had a year and a half to serve. His house was apparently furnished with some elegance, for there were *four* looking glasses (one was accounted a luxury) and a silk rug in addition to the more ususal silver spoons and furniture. He also owned a "Church Bible," but if this has survived the family record there (if any) has not been reported.[86]

John Tolson ordered a survey taken of all Butler Stonestreet's real property for the benefit of children in his care, and the following was recorded on 26 March 1761:

> "By virtue of appointment of Nathaniel Magruder one of His Lordship's Justices for the county aforesaid [Prince George's] and in persuance of an Act of Assembly of said Province. Relating to the Real Estate of orphan's. We do hereby Certify that we have entered upon the lands and Plantations of the Mr Butler Stonestreet now in the possession of Mr John Tolson in Behalf of the orphans of the said Stonestreet that is to say on Viewing the lands and plantations where the said Stonestreet lately lived we find thereon three clap Board Dwelling houses with Brick Chimneys and one Cellar one of which chimneys are ready to tumble down, five small out houses, two tobacco houses, one Dwelling House where is a tenement adjoining to the said Plantation and an orchard that contains about one hundred and fifty apple trees all of which are in Pretty Good Repair, and to adjudge the said lands Plantation and premises to be of the yearly value of £8 current money with the priviledge of Clearing one acre of the wood Land adjoining to the plantation yearly."

It continues with the number and condition of the dwellings and outbuildings at Littleworth (worth £3 10sh), Exeter (worth £6), and Wade's Adventure (worth £8), not repeated here. His house at Battersea was clapboarded but with brick chimneys, and was adorned with an orchard of about 150 apple trees. They produced, no doubt, the 360 gallons of cider on hand when his inventory had been taken.[87]

Children: (by his first wife)

i.   Sarah, born 1734. She married Richard Edelen (1715-1791) of Dublin (his ancestral home) in Piscataway Hundred, a brother of her stepmother. She survived him and was living in 1791.

ii.   Mary, born 1738. She married Humphrey Peake (1732-1785) of Fairfax County, Virginia. The Peakes were intimate friends of the Washingtons and were frequent dinner guests at

---

[85]Wills, book 30, pages 35-7. The original will survives, according to Harry Wright Newman, at the Hall of Records at Annapolis. It was proved by the oaths of Catherine Edelen, H. Addison, John Welling, and Alexander Fraser.

[86]Inventories, liber 60, folio 708.

[87]Prince George's County Deeds, book RR, page 126. It was taken by Alexander and William Norton, and produced at court on 6 February 1761.

Mount Vernon. She died 9 November 1805 "in the 67th year of her age" in Fairfax County.[88] She died at Gum Springs, and is buried there in the Peake Cemetery.

iii. Charity, born 1740. She died soon after her father, unmarried.

(by his second wife)

iv. Verlinda, born 12 April 1744. She married her cousin Butler Newman who was dead in 1790. She was living, his widow, in 1820.

v. Catherine, born 8 April 1747. She married firstly (in Virginia?) Samuel Johnson who died soon after leaving her with two young sons. She married secondly Benjamin Dicken in 1775. He died in 1794 in Edgecomb County, North Carolina. She survived him by many years and died in 1835.

vi. Elinor, born 4 April 1749. She is doubtless the *Nelly* Stonestreet over 45, enumerated alone (with five slaves) in that part of Prince George's County now the District of Columbia in the 1800 census.[89]

12. vii. Henry, born 11 September 1752.

13. viii. Richard, born 1754.

14. ix. Butler Edelen, born 8 February 1756.

7. EDWARD[3] STONESTREET of Battersea was born on 23 December 1705 in Piscataway Hundred, the son of Thomas (no. 3) and Christian (_____) Stonestreet. According to a great-grandson he married firstly Margaret Pye (a kinswoman), who appears by elimination to have been the daughter of Walter and Margaret (Faunt) Pye of St. John's Parish.[90] He married secondly Elinor, a daughter of Basil and Mary (_____) Williams, who had emigrated to America by 1748.[91] She was born about 1730 in South Wales,

---

[88]For the Peakes see *A Diary with reminiscences of the war and refugee life in the Shenandoah Valley, 1860-1865,* by Mrs Cornelia MacDonald (1934), page 446-9.

[89]*National Genealogical Society Quarterly,* volume 39, page 58 (June 1951).

[90]There does not seem to be any real reason to doubt this hearsay statement about Margaret (Pye) Stonestreet, although no proof of it has been found of it. Charles Edward Stonestreet (1844-1905) was a dedicated genealogist, and will be noticed later (family no. 49). Unfortunately his papers do not seem to have survived. However, on 10 October 1903 he wrote to his brother, an amateur poet, from Mount Clare, West Virginia, acknowledging the receipt of a poem and urging him to "try your hand again. That reminds me our Great Grandmother before marriage was Margaret Pye. Now if you will look in Chambers Cyclopedia, Volume 6th, page 56 you will find that a Poet Laureate, is an officer of the Household of the Sovereigns of Great Britain; and that Henry James Pye, was the 8th Officer that held the Office of Poet Laureate, to the Crown. And in Volume 9, page 7, your will find that in 1813, when James Pye died; the Great Poet Southey succeeded him as Poet Laureate. (Alfred Tennyson fills it now.) So, it would seem, that you have not acquired your taste for poetry from strangers." I am indebted to Albert L. Stonestreet of Houston, Texas, for a photocopy of this letter.

[91]Basil Williams settled briefly in Prince George's County, but moved soon after to near what is now Seneca in Montgomery County. On 7 September 1762 he had the lease of 300 acres from Lord Baltimore near the mouth of the Concocheaque, now Williamsport, where his eldest son Joseph had kept a tavern since 1752. Joseph Williams was the father of Brigadier-General Otho Holland Williams, the Revolutionary hero, who is buried at that place.

a sister of the Honorable Elisha Williams (1735-1812), whose daughter Mary married Elinor's son Butler Stonestreet.[92] The widow Stonestreet married before 11 February 1775 Ephraim Thorn (1733-1779) as her second husband, and Henry Duley (1731-1779) of Prince George's County was her third and final husband.[93] Edward Stonestreet (who was 25 years older than his second wife and the father of all her children) died in Prince George's County, Maryland, in 1771 (between 14 September and 28 November, the date and probate of his will).

Basil Williams, his second father-in-law, settled first in Prince Georges County, but then moved soon after to near Seneca in Sugarland Hundred in what became Montgomery County, Maryland. An interesting letter about this Williams family has survived, written by Simon Carson who was living in Frederick County, Virginia, in 1850 at the age of 81.[94] It was addressed to his son William Carson in the year 1849:

> "On the maternal side, your mama's father, E[lisha] Williams, was a Marylander and was a member of the Legislature when the Bill of Rights was formed, and perhaps until his removal to Virginia in the autumn of 1779. He had one sister [Elinor] who married [Edward] Stonestreet (your Uncle Butler Stonestreets father). After his death she married [Henry] Dooley. He had two brothers, John and Thomas. John married and went to Kentucky (where he left a large family). Thomas married a Miss [Elizabeth] Gibbs and died east of the [Blue] Ridge [in Loudoun County, Virginia]. His widow married Combs. Your grandma Williams was a [Ann] Swearingen -- her mothers maiden name Ray. She married at 16 years old to Swearingen 18 years old and lived together man and wife 84 years. One lived to be 100 and the other 102 years old. She had 15 children and raised 12 of them, who scatter a good deal over the U. S."[95]

The will of Edward Stonestreet was a fairly simple affair. It gave a slave named Sambo to his son Thomas and livestock to his son Joseph and daughter Christian Fry. Everything else, his dwelling, his plantation and land ("left me by my decd father") was bequeathed to his wife during her life and after her death it was to be divided among his seven children (or their heirs) who are named. Elinor was also appointed executrix.

His estate was appraised on 16 December 1771 by Robert Wade, Senior, and Edward Clarkson. It totalled £240 15sh 11d and lists John and Edward Stonestreet as his next of kin. Butler Newman and Elisha Lanham were bondsmen for Elinor Stonestreet in December 1771 when the will was entered for probate.

On 11 February 1775 Ephraim Thorn of Prince Georges County "having intermarried with Eleanor Stonestreet ... do bargain sell and deliver unto John Stonestreet and Edward Stonestreet, sons of the aforesaid Edward Stonestreet, deceased, and in behalf of themselves and the other children of the said

---

[92]Elinor was *not* the daughter of Christopher Edelen as is said in *Charles County Gentry* by Harry Wright Newman (1940), page 189.

[93]In the census of 1776 Henry Duley of Prince George's County was aged 45 and his first wife Mary was aged 39.

[94]The 1850 census of Frederick County, Virginia, page 342.

[95]Copy supplied by Marian Boyd of Williamsburg, Virginia. There are further particulars on both the Carson and Williams family. I have added the material found in square backets in the excerpt quoted above to reinforce Mr. Carson's memory.

Edward Stonestreet" personal property belonging to their father. It included slaves named Jack, James and Pinder (a negro woman), three feather beds and furniture, a horse, six head of cattle, seven sheep, twelve hogs, a table and six chairs, a chest, three iron pots and other furniture in the house.[96]

Ephraim Thorn left a will dated 31 May 1779 leaving his entire estate to his wife Elinor. At her death or marriage all of his estate was to go to his "son-in-law" (for which we must read *stepson*) Thomas Stonestreet. It was proved on 25 October 1779.[97]

The slaves belonging to Edward Stonestreet were apparently transported to Loudoun County, Virginia, where several of his sons settled. On 11 June 1801 the heirs of Christian Fry (formerly Stonestreet), the heirs of Joseph Stonestreet, John Stonestreet, the heirs of Edward Stonestreet, and Butler Stonestreet (all heirs of Edward Stonestreet, Senior) brought a suit in Loudoun County against Basil and Thomas Stonestreet who seem to have had the slaves in their possession. The court found that the representatives of Edward, Jr., had received more than his share of his fathers slaves, and they ordered that the remainder of them be divided into six equal parts for distribution to the remaining heirs.[98] On 13 July 1801 the commissioners reported that slaves named Penny, Lydia, Amy, Anne, Sam, Jerry, Jack and Moses valued at £360 had been divided (with certain cash adjustments) into six equal shares for the heirs.[99]

Battersea was conveyed by the heirs of Edward Stonestreet, the elder, by a series of quitclaim deeds to their cousin Richard Stonestreet who had another part of the tract already by the devise of his father. Verlinda and Mary Lanham, daughters of Christian (Stonestreet) Lanham Fry, then the wives of John Allen and John Frazer conveyed their one-fourteenth interest (half of their mothers one-seventh) on 25 November 1800 and 15 May 1801 to Richard Stonestreet.[100]

Children: (by his first wife)

| | i. | Christian, born 1730. She married firstly (about 1760) Eleazer Lanham, and secondly (by 1771) Leonard Trueman Fry. She was dead before 25 November 1800. |
| 15. | ii. | Joseph, born 1740. |

(by his second wife)

16.	iii.	John, born 1751.
17.	iv.	Edward, baptized 14 January 1753.
18.	v.	Basil Williams, born 18 March 1755.
19.	vi.	Butler, born 5 November 1757.
20.	vii.	Thomas, born about 1763.

---

[96]Prince George's County Deeds, book CC, page 90.
[97]Prince George's County Wills, book T, page 118.
[98]Loudoun County, Virginia, Orders, book 4, page 391.
[99]Ibid., page 415.
[100]Verlinda Lanham married John Allen on 29 October 1781 and Mary Lanham married John Frazier on 24 October 1789 in Prince Georges County. The sisters and their husbands were all living in 1800. For an account of Edward Stonestreet and his Lanham granddaughters see the *Maryland Genealogical Society Bulletin*, vol. 38, no. 1 (Winter 1997) 16.

FOURTH GENERATION

8. BUTLER[4] STONESTREET was born 20 October 1748 in Trinity Parish, Charles County, the son of Butler (no. 5) and Elizabeth (Freeman) Stonestreet. He had died, a bachelor, before 20 November 1784 when an inventory was taken of his estate.

He and his brother Edward were the only two Stonestreets in the 1775 census of Charles County; both were living in East Newport Hundred.[101] He served as administrator of his mother Elizabeth Stonestreet in 1776.

He and his brother Edward served in the American Revolution in Captain John Parnham's company of the 12th Battalion of Maryland Militia.[102]

The personal estate of Butler Stonestreet, deceased, was appraised on 20 November 1784 at £116 14sh 6d, and was filed on 19 February 1785. He was a tobacco planter but no real property is mentioned in the probate. John Winter and Thomas Ching were bondsmen for Edward Stonestreet.

The receipts for the vendue sale of the personal estate of the deceased brought only £89 8sh 11d. Edward Stonestreet reported an expense of 13sh 6d for liquor dispensed at the sale. Also itemized were debts owing to the estate and the value of his crops. After all the obligations against the estate were paid a balance of £143 15sh 2d remained for distribution among the five brothers and sisters of Butler Stonestreet. Edward, Thomas and James F. Stonestreet, together with their sisters Elizabeth Mattingly and Mary Swann each received £28 15sh 0d.[103]

9. EDWARD[4] STONESTREET was born on 6 January 1754 in Trinity Parish, Charles County, the son of Butler (no. 5) and Elizabeth (Freeman) Stonestreet. He married Anne, the daughter of William and Elinor (Wilkinson) McPherson.[104] She was born 1 November 1757 and married as her second husband Alexander King on 14 January 1798 at St. Johns Church at Piscataway. Edward Stonestreet died in 1796 (between 21st October and 29th November).

He served with his brother Butler Stonestreet in Captain John Parnham's company of the 12th Battalion of the Maryland Militia in the American Revolution.[105]

---

[101]Brumbaugh, *Maryland Records* I, 302.

[102]The muster roll is printed in the *National Genealogical Society Quarterly*, volume 32 (September 1944), pages 68-9.

[103]Wills, liber AH no. 9, folio 162.

[104]For the McPherson family of Charles County see the *Maryland Historical Magazine,* volume 1, pages 347-8.

[105]His name is wrongly transcribed as *Leonard* Stonestreet in the printed copy of the muster roll in the *National Genealogical Society Quarterly*.

He was enumerated in the first census of Maryland in 1790 as the head of a household in Charles County that included a wife and a young son and daughter.[106]

His will is dated 21 October 1796 when he was "weak in body." He requested his executors to "omit a sermon with all other pomp" at his funeral. His slaves were to be hired out to the best advantage and the profit from this used for the maintenance and education of his three children. His children were to have a featherbed and furniture each and the rest of his personal property was to be sold. Curiously there is no mention in the will of his wife, but her McPherson brothers and a sister were named his executors.[107]

The will was proved on 29 November 1796 and Charles McPherson was granted administration on 3 December 1796 with Walter McPherson and John Hoskins Boarman as sureties in the sum of £1000. Karren McPherson and Mary McPherson renounced their right as executrixes. The vendue sale of his personal effects produced sales totalling £279 6sh 11d and it was recorded in December 1797 at the orphans court.

His children were heirs of their spinster aunt Karenhappock McPherson. Elizabeth Stonestreet gave a receipt on 25 September 1813 for her share of the estate to John Cooksey, and three days later Mary McPherson acknowledged that she had received the share belonging to John Stonestreet.[108]

       Children: (the eldest son, adopted)

21.   i.   Benjamin.

               (by his wife Anne McPherson)

      ii.   Elizabeth, born 1785. She married Henry H. Turner of Charles County and was living in 1838.
22. iii.   William, born 1790.
23. iv.   Charles, born July 1792.

10. THOMAS[4] STONESTREET was born at an unrecorded date in Trinity Parish, Charles County, the son of Butler (no. 5) and Elizabeth (Freeman) Stonestreet. He died before 22 August 1797, a bachelor, in Charles County, Maryland.

On 31 January 1795 he had a mortgage on 100 acres, part of a tract called Lapworth Enlarged, from his first cousin Robert Slye of Charles County for £57 5sh.[109] If Slye repaid this sum with legal interest from 2 February 1795 by 1 January 1797, then this mortgage was to be revoked.

His will is dated 23 November 1796 when he was "infirm of body." All of his personal property (except

[106]*Heads of families 1790...Maryland* (1907), page 53.
[107]Charles County Wills, 1791-1808, page 368.
[108]Charles County Wills, 1791-1808, page 368.
[109]Charles County Deeds, book N-4, page 358. Robert Slye III was born on 15 November 1745 according to the register of Trinity Church.

his clothes and gun) was to be sold and money invested. If Thomas, the son of Francis Brown, lived until 1 July 1813 (presumably his 21st birthday) then the money was to be delivered to him. If Thomas Brown died before 1813 then the money was to go to his nephew William Stonestreet. His brother James Freeman Stonestreet was to have his wearing apparel and his gun. The will was probated on 22 August 1797.[110]

Thomas Brown was apparently the illegitimate son of Thomas Stonestreet. He was still living on 24 July 1806 when Nathaniel Freeman (1733-1807) left him a horse, saddle and bridle worth $45.00 "in consideration and as an acknowledgement of favors which I think I received from a certain Thomas Stonestreet his reputed father in his lifetime."[111] How long Thomas Brown lived after this date is unknown.

11. JAMES FREEMAN[4] STONESTREET was born in Trinity Parish, Charles County, Maryland, the youngest son of Butler (no. 5) and Elizabeth (Freeman) Stonestreet. He married Anne _____ who was born in 1780; she survived him and had married secondly Elijah Smith in Fauquier County, Virginia, by 1816. James F. Stonestreet died just previous to 26 March 1808 in Fauquier County.

He had moved to Leeds Parish in Fauquier County by 1798, the first year in which he appears as a tithable. He had not inherited any land in Maryland and it is not surprising to find that he moved to Virginia where he settled on a promising plantation.[112] He appears last in the tax list of 1807 when he paid for three slaves over 16 and three horses. In 1809 his widow Anne Stonestreet was the head of a household with the same number of slaves and horses.[113]

The inventory of his estate was taken on 26 March 1808 and appraised at $1287.00. A vendue sale was not held until 1816 when the widow and her second husband purchased much of Stonestreet's personal property. The estate was finally settled on 25 March 1817.

In 1810 Elijah Smith was the head of a family in Fauquier County that apparently included his five Stonestreet stepchildren; with him were a male and female 10 to 16, and two males and a female under 10. He had four slaves according to the enumeration.[114]

The estate of James Freeman Stonestreet was eventually divided into sixths. Each heir was first paid $62.93, and then later another payment of $135.00. The share of his fathers slaves belonging to Hezekiah Stonestreet was sold by decree of the court, as he was judged incompetent.[115]

Elijah and Anne Smith, aged 68 and 70, were living in the First District of Fauquier County in 1850. Hezekiah Stonestreet, aged 53, was still living at home.[116]

    Children:

---

[110]Charles County Wills, 1791-1808, page 410.

[111]Ibid., page 46-57.

[112]Personal Tax Lists, Virginia State Library. Leeds Parish was the northern half of the county.

[113]Ibid. His slaves Peter, Mary and Burrell are named in the inventory of his estate.

[114]The 1810 census of Fauquier County, Virginia, page 406.

[115]Fauquier County Wills, book 4, page 465.

[116]The 1850 census of Fauquier County, Virginia, page 216.

24.	i.	Butler, born 1795.
	ii.	Hezekiah, born 1797. He was living unmarried with his mother and stepfather in 1850.
	iii.	Elizabeth, born 1799. She married Thomas Dever on 30 January 1816 in Frederick County, Virginia.
25.	iv.	George Washington.
	v.	Jane, living unmarried in 1817. She married William Patton on 1 May 1828 in adjoining Culpeper County, Virginia. [Her name was formerly misread as *James* by Harry Wright Newman, a major confusion as James Freeman Stonestreet had no son of this name to survive him.]
26.	vi.	Thomas, born 19 April 1806.

12. HENRY[4] STONESTREET of Cornwallis' Neck in Charles County, Maryland, was born 11 September 1752 the son of Butler (no. 6) and Jane (Edelen) Stonestreet. He married his cousin Mary Noble Edelen, a daughter of James and Salome (Noble) Edelen. She was born in 1753 and died in 1818. Henry Stonestreet was dead before 18 August 1812 when his widow renounced her right to administer his estate.

Henry Stonestreet was a guest of Martha and George Washington at dinner at Mt. Vernon on 18 December 1771 together with his sister Mary and her husband Humphrey Peake according to an entry in Washington's diary.[117]

On 4 December 1774 he requested the Land Commission to survey three tracts called Battersea, Littleworth, and Athley's Folly; all were in Prince Georges County and had formerly belonged to Butler Stonestreet about 37 or 38 years previously according to his petition.[118]

In 1776 he and his wife, newly married, were enumerated in a census of Prince George's County in St. George's Parish. He was aged 24 and his wife 23, and they were living alone with 14 slaves.[119]

He was a patriot early in the Revolution and took the oath of fidelity and support in Prince Georges County on 27 January 1778. He served throughout the war as Adjutant General to the Maryland Militia and there are abundant references to payments made to him as his salary and for accounts he had rendered to the Maryland Council.[120]

Henry Stonestreet was living by 3 September 1796 in Charles County when he conveyed to Dr. James Edelen his plantation called Cornwallis' Neck.[121] Dr. Edelen died a bachelor at the age of 60, and his will dated 13 August 1813 was proved in Prince Georges County. His heirs included two sisters Mary and Margaret Stonestreet.[122] Cornwallis' Neck may only have been mortgaged (or a life interest given) to Dr. Edelen for Henry Stonestreet continued to reside there until his death. On 3 March 1831 Nicholas Stonestreet sold 368 acres, part of Cornwallis' Neck, to Charles A. Pye. It was all the real property his

---

[117]*Diaries of George Washington 1748-1799* (1925), II, 46.
[118]Prince George's County Deeds, book CC-2, page 55.
[119]Brumbaugh, *Maryland Records*, I, 85.
[120]*Maryland Archives*, volume 12, page 262; volume 16, pages 54, 245, 421; volume 21, page 215.
[121]Harry Wright Newman, *Charles County Gentry* (1940), page 178.
[122]Prince George's County Wills, book TT no. 1, page 80.

father had owned except for a part of the tract which had already been set off for Joseph N. Stonestreet. On 21 December 1831 Pye sold the tract to his brother John A. Pye and the deed notes that it was the "land and plantation on which Henry Stonestreet lived and died & which descended to his children at his death intestate."[123]

In 1810 Henry Stonestreet was head of a large household at Cornwallis' Neck in St. Georges Parish (Pomonkey) in Charles County which included 37 slaves.[124] His son Joseph Noble Stonestreet lived on an adjoining tract.

He had died before 18 August 1812 when *Nancy* [sic] Stonestreet renounced her claim and title to administer the estate of her late husband Henry Stonestreet. She asked the court to appoint her sons Joseph Noble and Nicholas Stonestreet as administrators. The court obliged and they posed a bond of £5000 on the same day.[125]

Mary Stonestreet, his widow, died testate in 1818 (will dated 3 September, proved 7 December). She bequeathed an enormous number of slaves to her children and grandchildren. Her sons Joseph Noble and Nicholas were to have her large dining table, six leather chairs, and her silver and china. Provision was also made for the children of Lewis Stonestreet if he "should Marry and have Lawful issue."[126]

Children:

27. i.   Dr. Henry, born 18 September 1776.
28. ii. Dr. James Edelen, born about 1778. He died, a bachelor, at Annapolis, Maryland, on 19 September 1805 in his 25th year and is buried there.
29. iii. Joseph Noble, born about 1780.
30. iv. Nicholas, born 25 September 1782.
        v.   Jane. She married firstly Joseph Neale (died 1804), and secondly Henry Digges. Her will was proved 31 August 1832.[127]
31. vi. Lewis.
        vii. Mary Noble. She was living unmarried on 9 August 1814 when she was an heir of her uncle Richard Stonestreet, but had died before 3 September 1818.

13. CAPTAIN RICHARD[4] STONESTREET of Battersea at Piscataway was born 26 May 1754 the son of Butler (no. 6) and Jane (Edelen) Stonestreet. He married firstly Ann, the daughter of John and Ann (Lowe) Tolson.[128] IIc married secondly (in or soon after 1776) Margaret, the daughter of James and Salome (Noble) Edelen, and a sister to the wife of his brother Henry Stonestreet. Richard Stonestreet died before

[123]Charles County Deeds, book IB-19, page 470.
[124]The census of 1810 of Charles County, Maryland, page 342.
[125]Charles County Orphan's Court, 1812-4, page 63.
[126]Charles County Wills, 1818-1825, page 41.
[127]For her posterity see Harry Wright Newman, *The Maryland Semmes and kindred families* (1956), pages 318, 322.
[128]*Maryland Genealogical Society Bulletin*, vol. 20, no. 2 (Spring 1979) 124. Note that both Francis and John Tolson married ladies named Ann Lowe.

28 April 1815 (the date his will was probated) in Prince George's County, Maryland.

In 1776 Richard Stonestreet (aged 22) and his wife Ann (age 18) were living in St. John's Parish with 11 slaves.[129] Nearby was Salome Edelen, a widow, with her daughter Margaret (age 20) who was to become the second wife of Richard Stonestreet.

On 9 March 1778 Richard Stonestreet took the oath of fidelity and support in Prince George's County.[130] Later in the same year he was commissioned as a Second Lieutenant in the militia, and was subsequently promoted to Captain.[131]

He had no surviving children by either of his wives. In 1800 he and Margaret were living alone at Battersea with 22 slaves.[132]

His will is dated 9 October 1814 when he was weak in body. His wife Margaret was to have all his real and personal property during her life. After her death his nephew Henry Stonestreet was to have his land. His brother Butler was left a legacy of $500.00. His faithful man Charles was given his freedom. Slaves were left to his niece Jane Digges, his nephew Joseph N. Stonestreet, his nephew Lewis Stonestreet, his niece Mary N[oble] Stonestreet, and a grandnephew and niece Charles Henry Stonestreet and Mary Olivia Stonestreet.[133] The residue of his estate was left to his nephew Nicholas Stonestreet.[134]

14. BUTLER EDELEN[4] STONESTREET of Wade's Adventure was born on 8 February 1756 (and christened 29 February 1756) the posthumous son of Butler (no. 6) and Jane (Edelen) Stonestreet. He married Sarah, who was born on 20 January 1759, the eldest daughter of William and Elinor (_____) Norton at Upper Marlborough in Prince George's County, Maryland, on 6 January 1778. She was born 15 January 1757 (according to her tombstone) in Prince George's County, Maryland, and died 26 November 1824 "age 67 lacking one month 24 days."[135] They are buried in the Stonestreet Cemetery on Kentucky State Route 146 in Oldham County, Kentucky.

He served in the American Revolution enlisting on 15 July 1776 in Prince George's County. He was enrolled by Ensign Horatio Claggett subject to review by Lieutenant Colonel John Addison.

On 30 December 1778 he sold Wade's Adventure which he had inherited from his father to John Baynes

---

[129]Brumbaugh, *Maryland Records*, I, 57.
[130]Ibid., II, 279.
[131]*Maryland Archives*, volume 12, page 186; volume 16, page 356.
[132]The 1800 census of Prince George's County, page 445.
[133]Charles Henry was to have a negro boy named Ben, and his sister Olivia (who seems to have died soon after) a Negro girl named Fanny.
[134]Prince George's County Wills, 1808-1854, page 116.
[135]The register of St. John's Piscataway gives her date of birth as 20 January 1759, which is more likely to be correct. Her mother Elinor Norton is sometimes said to have been a Stonestreet, but no proof of this can be found. Elinor Norton was born about 1738 (aged 38 in 1776) and there is no lost Elinor Stonestreet born in this period.

for £250.[136] It contained 115 acres and his wife Sarah surrendered her dower on the same day.

They went soon after to Pittsylvania County, Virginia, with the Norton family. Butler Stonestreet appears on the tax list for 1785 in Pittsylvania County with five white souls, no dwelling (but with three other buildings).[137] He and the Nortons were then living along the Dan River. On 18 April 1785 he had a bill of sale from Moses Vincent in Pittsylvania County and he was still there on 21 July 1794 when he sold personal property to Benjamin Thomas.[138]

Butler Edelen Stonestreet apparently moved in the same year to Rowan County, North Carolina. He had bought 185 acres there on the west side of Muddy Creek for £164 on 11 April 1793 from William Poole, Senior, of Rowan County.[139] On 7 November 1794 he gave a bond with Jonathan Markland and Lewis Mullican at the probate of the will of his cousin Edward Stonestreet. Butler is identified as a constable. On 25 January 1799 Butler Stonestreet of Rowan County sold 60 acres on the west side of Muddy Creek for £60 to John Brown of Warren County, North Carolina.[140] He was still in Rowan County at the time of the 1800 census.[141]

Butler and Sarah Stonestreet sold all of their land (204 acres) on 21 February 1801 to John Burkhart for $800.00 and moved to Iredell County, North Carolina.[142] He purchased 335 acres there on the waters of Third Creek on 26 February 1802 from James McGinty for $750.00.[143] He added other tracts to his holdings on Third Creek and sold a parcel there on 20 February 1809 to Nathaniel Brown, his son-in-law.[144] He was enumerated in the 1810 census of Iredell County.[145]

By 1814 he and his son Henry Stonestreet were taxed in the Pewee Valley near Floydsburg (then Jefferson County, Kentucky) in what became Oldham County in 1823. In 1817 he had 100 acres on Floyd's Fork, nine slaves and six horses in Jefferson County. (Henry, his son, was taxed on one slave and three horses.)[146] He was there at the time of the 1820 census.[147]

On 11 October 1823 he was back in Iredell County where he sold 230 acres (a part of the property bought from James McGinty) to Ethelred Ellis for $450.00.[148]

He is last taxed in Jefferson County, Kentucky, in 1822. In 1825 he was taxed in Oldham County, newly

---

[136]Prince George's County Deeds, book CC-2, page 558.
[137]Personal Tax List, Virginia State Library.
[138]Pittsylvania County Deeds, book 7, page 431; book 10, page 33.
[139]Rowan County Deeds, book 13, page 396. He purchased another 79 acres on Muddy Creek on 1 April 1795 (book 14, page 103.)
[140]Ibid., book 17, page 365.
[141]The 1800 census of Rowan County, North Carolina, page 362.
[142]Rowan County Deeds, book 17, page 607.
[143]Iredell County Deeds, book E, page 1.
[144]Ibid., book F, page 193; book G, page 82.
[145]The 1810 census of Iredell County, page 22.
[146]Personal Tax Lists, Kentucky Historical Society.
[147]The 1820 census of Jefferson County, Kentucky, page 61.
[148]Iredell County Deeds, book L, page 276

formed, with his son Henry.[149]

The will of Butler Stonestreet, Senior, of Oldham County, Kentucky, was dated 24 January 1825. Butler was "of weak state." His will is very simple; it leaves all his estate, his dwelling, plantation, household furniture, and his stock to his youngest son Butler. He mentions earlier gifts to his older children Anne White, Elizabeth Brown, Mary Isaac, his sons Richard and Henry, and Sarah Fetheringill. His son Butler was to pay $2.00 yearly to the Methodist Church "for the use of the Gospel by me." His will was proved 19 June 1826.[150]

Children:

	i.	Anne. She married _____ White.
	ii.	Elizabeth, born 22 August 1780. She married Nathaniel B. Brown, and died 25 October 1850 age 70 years, two months, and three days. She is buried in the Floydsburg Cemetery in Oldham County, Kentucky.
	iii.	Mary. She married Richard Augustus Wilkes Isaacs (1774-1845). She died in 1812.
32.	iv.	Richard born 1785.
33.	v.	Henry, born 1789.
34.	vi.	Butler, born 6 October 1797.
	vii.	Sarah, born 19 August 1799. She married Elias Fetheringill on 27 August 1818 in Jefferson County, Kentucky. They lived in Oldham County, Kentucky.

15. JOSEPH⁴ STONESTREET was born in 1740, the eldest son of Edward (no. 7) and Margaret (Pye) Stonestreet. He married Alice _____ (who was born about 1748) in the 1770s in Prince George's County. He was probably dead in or before 1790, and beyond any doubt in 1801, and nothing has been learned of his widow.

Joseph Stonestreet is enumerated in 1776 in a census of Prince George's County, aged 36, with his wife Alice, aged 28, and another female aged one (his daughter Mary Ann, no doubt).[151] He took the Oath of Fidelity and Support in the same county on 1 March 1778.[152] He is not found in the 1790 census of Maryland, and was presumably dead by that date.

It seems likely (but unproven) that his son Walter was named for his grandfather Pye.

On 13 July 1801 a slave named Moses valued at £45 (and a money payment of an additional £12 10sh 1 1/2d) was allotted in Loudoun County, Virginia, to the unnamed heirs of Joseph Stonestreet as their share of the slaves of Edward Stonestreet, Senior. Moses appears to have been sold to Basil Stonestreet who left him in his will dated 18 November 1810 to his daughter Sarah Stonestreet.[153]

---

[149]Oldham County Tax Lists, Kentucky Historical Society. It is possible that the Butler Stonestreet assessed this year in Oldham County was his son Butler Sonestreet, Junior.
[150]Oldham County Wills, book 1, page 60.
[151]Brumbaugh, *Maryland Records*, I, 75.
[152]Ibid., II, 290.
[153]Loudoun County Wills, book 1, page 373.

His father Edward remembered him in his will of 14 September 1771 with a heifer three years old. He (or his heirs) would also have had a one-seventh interest in Battersea, but no deeds are on record concerning his share of the plantation.

Children: (perhaps incomplete)

    i.   Mary Ann, born 16 April 1776 according to the register of St. John's Church at Piscataway.

35. ii.   Edward, born about 1780-4.

    iii.   Walter, born 1780-90. He appears to have married Elizabeth _____ (born about 1795). They were living in 1820 in Loudoun County, Virginia, both aged 26 to 45, with another female over 45.[154] He is not found indexed anywhere in 1830, but in 1840 he was living in Frederick County, Virginia, age 50 to 60 with a female age 40 to 50. They seemingly had no children, and he is not found in the 1850 census. [It probable that the Elizabeth Stonestreet aged 55 who was living in adjoining Berkeley County (now West Virginia) in 1850 with James McConnell (aged 61) was his widow. James McConnell was unmarried in 1850, and Elizabeth Stonestreet, perhaps a sister, was keeping house for him.]

16. ENSIGN JOHN[4] STONESTREET was born in 1751 a son of Edward (no. 7) and Elinor (Williams) Stonestreet. He married about 1772 Ann (Nancy) Finley; she was born in 1757 the daughter of _____ and Elinor (Timberlake) Finley. She married Abraham Fulkerson as her second husband on 24 February 1807. Ann died on 13 August 1831, aged 74, and is buried beside her first husband in the Stonestreet Cemetery in Jessamine County, Kentucky. John Stonestreet died in the spring of 1802.

The earliest mention yet found to John Stonestreet is in December 1771 when he accepted the executorship of his grandfather Thomas Stonestreet. John Stonestreet would have just come of age by this date, and Butler Newman and Jonathan Burk served as his bondmen.

John had married Ann Finley by 1772 in Prince George's County if the 1776 census is to be trusted in the matter of ages, since they had two daughters aged four in that year.[155] John was 25 and his wife Ann was 19. There are also three unidentified females aged 28, 26, and 18 living in his household in 1776.[156]

John Stonestreet embraced the Revolutionary cause early in the war. On 24 May 1776 the Council of Safety ordered that he be paid £3 13sh 2d "on [the] Account of North Carolina Prisoners" apparently in the custody of John Stonestreet.[157]

In 1777 he was commissioned an Ensign in the company commanded by his cousin Captain Richard

---

[154]In addition to the census of 1820 he was taxed earlier in the same year on 23 March 1820 in Loudoun County. (List C of the Personal Property Tax List of Loudoun County.) Close attention to his neighbors on the twenty-third might pin down his abode in the county.

[155]Brumbaugh, *Maryland Records,* I, 76. Only the birth of Elizabeth on 27 March 1773 is found recorded at St. John's Church in Piscataway. Presumably her sister Elinor was a year or so younger.

[156]Ibid.

[157]*Maryland Archives*, volume xi, page 441.

Stonestreet.[158] He took the oath of fidelity and support in Prince Georges County on 27 January 1778.[159]

He was on the point of moving to Virginia on 22 March 1780 when Thomas Lewis, Senior, Thomas Lewis, Junior, and William Lewis, all of Loudoun County, sold to John Stonestreet of Prince Georges County, 200 acres on Difficult Run, the stream that divided Fairfax County from Loudoun until 1798.[160] The Lewis family of Loudoun County were old friends (very possibly kinsman) from Maryland. He and his brother Basil Stonestreet first appear on the 1782 tax list of Loudoun County, Virginia. John Stonestreet is taxed on two polls (the other may have been his brother Thomas) and seven slaves. Both he and his brother Thomas taught school in Loudoun County.

John Stonestreet was a witness in Fairfax County, Virginia, on 1 January 1792 to the will of Henry Gunnell of that place. He moved about 1795 to Kentucky (when his son James was aged eight) and was a witness in Fayette County, Kentucky, on 29 June 1798 to the will of John Lawson.[161] He was taxed in 1800 in Jessamine County (recently formed from Fayette) where he died two years later.

His will is dated 1 March 1802 and was proved at the May sitting of the court. His wife Ann was to have his plantation of 150 acres, three slaves named Nace, Jenny and Sam, his household furniture and provisions, certain livestock and a bond due from Christopher Supinger. His son John Dent Stonestreet was left three negroes named Ben, Pat and Phillis, a sorrel mare, and a bond due from John Peniston. His daughter Nelly (already married to Cornelius Darnaby) was to have three slaves in her possession (Judah, Pen and Lewis) and a fourth named Anney at her mothers death. She was also confirmed in a mare, cattle and household furniture already in her possession. James Stonestreet was to have three negroes named Hannah, Bob and Sal, a colt worth £20, cattle and household furniture. At the death of his wife his plantation was to be divided between his sons, and the personal property left to the widow was to be divided among his three children. Jenny, a favored slave, was given the boon of choosing which of his children she preferred to live with. The widow Ann took an oath as executrix and posted a bond of £2500.[162]

Ann Stonestreet married Abraham Fulkerson, a widower with six children, soon after. He left a will dated 6 April 1812 in Jessamine County which remembers his wife Ann, his three sons and three married daughters, and his stepson Stonestreet.[163]

---

[158]Ibid., volume xxi, page 62.

[159]Brumbaugh, *Maryland Records,* II, 265.

[160]Loudoun County Deeds, book N, page 197-200. The complete text of this deed will also be found in *Virginia County Court Records, Deed Abstracts of Loudoun County, Virginia 1779-1782* (McLean, Virginia, 1990) 58-9. The deed was acknowledged on 9 April 1781 (Orders, book G, page 329) with the notation that the "Feme" (unnamed) had relinquished her dower. Thomas Lewis, Junior, went to Nelson County, Kentucky, by 1788 and on 9 June 1788 a deed of gift from Thomas Lewis to his son Daniel was proved by the oath of John Stonestreet (Orders, book K, page 457).

[161]See B. F. Van Meter, *Genealogies and sketches of some old families who have taken a prominent part in the development of Virginia and Kentucky,* page 73, for a memoir of James Stonestreet, and the *William and Mary Quarterly,* series 1, volume 23, page 68, for an abstract of the Lawson will.

[162]Jessamine County Wills, book A, page 48.

[163]Ibid., page 434.

Children:

	i.	Elizabeth, born 27 March 1773. She was living in 1776 but died young, probably unmarried.
	ii.	Elinor (Nelly). She married Cornelius Darnaby on 24 March 1801 in Jessmamine County.
36.	iii.	John Dent.
37.	iv.	James, born 1 October 1787.

17. EDWARD[4] STONESTREET was born in Prince George's County, Maryland, probably at the end of 1752, and was baptized on 14 January 1753 the son of Edward (no. 7) and Elinor (Williams) Stonestreet. He married Margery Weight on 14 May 1780 in Prince George's County, and died in 1794 in Rowan (that part now Davie) County, North Carolina. His widow Margery survived in Rowan County until 1825.

Edward Stonestreet took the oath of fidelity and loyalty in Prince George's County on 23 February 1778.[164] He went soon after to Rowan County, North Carolina, where he witnessed a deed on 11 August 1786 and was taxed in 1787 having "in all 6 soles" including one slave.

He was enumerated there in Salisbury district in the first census of 1790 with two males over 16, two males under 16, four females, and one slave.[165]

Edward Stonestreet was dead, aged about 42, before 7 November 1794 when his will was exhibited for probate in Rowan County. It was rejected (and is now lost) as the witnesses were not willing to swear that he was of sound mind when it was signed. Margery Stonestreet qualified as administrator and gave a bond of £500 with Basil Gaither and Isaac Jones as her securities. The inventory of the estate and the account of sales were filed on 7 August 1795.

Margery Stonestreet survived her husband by many years. She never remarried and the administration of her own estate was given on 21 November 1825 to her son Elisha. He was given permission on the same day to sell a slave named Will belonging to his mother and gave bond in the amount of $600.[166] Margery and her son Elisha Stonestreet were heads of families in 1810 in Rowan County.[167]

Children:

38.	i.	Elisha.
39.	ii.	John R., born 1785.
	iii.	Elinor. She married Richmond Gilpin, Senior, on 15 February 1811. They removedd to Fayette County, Alabama, where she is listed as blind in the 1860 census.
	iv.	Nancy. She married John Bailey on 10 August 1811.
40.	v.	Benjamin.

---

[164]Brumbaugh, *Maryland Records,* II, 287. "Rezen" Harbin who took the oath at the same time also went to North Carolina.

[165]*Heads of Families...North Carolina* (1907), page 171.

[166]Rowan County Court Minutes, court held on Monday, 21 November 1825.

[167]The 1810 census of Rowan County, North Carolina, page 284.

18. BASIL WILLIAMS⁴ STONESTREET was born 18 March 1755 the son of Edward (no. 7) and Elinor (Williams) Stonestreet of Prince George's County, Maryland. He married about 1775 Elizabeth, who was born in 1757 and may have been a daughter of _____ Smallwood. She was living as late as 1830 in Cameron Parish, Loudoun County, Virginia. Basil W. Stonestreet had died in Loudoun County before 10 June 1811 when his will was proved.

Basil Williams Stonestreet presumably married about 1775; in the 1776 census he was aged 21 (which agrees perfectly with the date of birth entered in the register of St. Johns Church) and his wife Elizabeth was aged 19. Also in the household was a female aged nine months (presumably their daughter Ann Williams Stonestreet) and three slaves.[168]

John Ballard Barker signed his will on 12 June 1777 in Charles County. The witnesses included an Elizabeth Smallwood Stonestreet who (for want of any competition) we assume to have been the same Elizabeth who was wife of Basil W. Stonestreet.[169]

In 1782 Basil Stonestreet was taxed in Loudoun County, Virginia, with one poll (himself) and four slaves.[170] He was in Loudoun County in 1810 with a household that included himself and his wife (both over 45), two sons aged 16-26, and a daughter aged 16-26 (probably Sarah, who was still unmarried). Insofar as slaves were any measure of wealth he was apparently in comfortable circumstances, with 13 negroes on the plantation.

His will is dated later in the same year on 18 November 1810. To his daughter Sarah Stonestreet he left a tract of about 150 acres purchased from Ludwell Lee. She was also to have three slaves named Moses, Liddy and Patty. His son Benjamin Asa Stonestreet was to have two Negro boys named Sam and *Chales* [sic] and a colt. Augustus Stonestreet was to have slaves named Billy and Harry and a colt. His daughter Ann Jones was to have a slave named Rachel and her child.

He also set up a trust for his daughter Elizabeth Blincoe to be managed by his friend (actually son-in-law) Henry Jones and his son Benjamin Asa Stonestreet. His negroes Patient, Bill and James and $200.00 were to be held by the trustees for the benefit of Mrs. Blincoe and her children. All the rest of his estate went to the widow and executrix. At her death all his land (except that devised to his daughter Sarah) was to be sold and the money divided among his children and grandchildren. His will was proved on 10 June 1811 and ordered to be recorded.[171]

Children:

i.   Hannah (Ann) Williams, born 20 October 1775. She married Henry Jones on 8 January 1798 in Loudoun County with the written consent of her father Basil Williams Stonestreet. They had moved by 1806 to Bath County, Virginia. On 10 October 1815 Hannah Jones and Butler Stonestreet gave a bond for $200.00 in Bath County for Hannah to serve as the

---

[168]Brumbaugh, *Maryland Records,* I, 26.
[169]Charles County Wills, book 7, page 52. A full text of the will has not been seen.
[170]Personal Tax Lists, Virginia State Library.
[171]Loudoun County Wills, book 1, page 373.

executor of Henry Jones. She never remarried and died there in 1850.

    ii.   Sarah. She married Walter H. Dorsett on 22 December 1819 in Montgomery County, Maryland. He brought a suit in chancery against his mother-in-law Elizabeth Stonestreet in 1839 in Loudoun County.[172]

41.   iii.   Benjamin Asa.
42.   iv.   Augustus, born 1788.
      v.   Elizabeth. She married _____ Blincoe.

19. BUTLER[4] STONESTREET was born on 5 November 1757 in Prince George's County, Maryland, the son of Edward (no. 7) and Elinor (Williams) Stonestreet. He married firstly his cousin Mary who had been christened on 4 November 1759 at Prince Georges Parish, the daughter of the Honorable Elisha and Ann (Swearingen) Williams. She was the mother of all of his children. He married secondly, in old age, Phebe Akeman, a daughter of William Akeman of Bath County, Virginia. She was previously the widow of firstly Richard Mayse, Senior (whom she had married on 5 August 1799 with her brother John Akeman as surety), and later of Simon Minnick. Butler Stonestreet and the widow Phebe Minnick were married on 13 June 1830 in Bath County. Butler died there in 1836.

His father-in-law Elisha Williams, who was born in South Wales in 1735, had represented the Lower District of Frederick County (now Montgomery County) in the Maryland House of Delegates.

He had moved by 1776 to Georgetown Hundred, Frederick County, Maryland, where he is enumerated in the census of that year. His future wife Mary (aged 16) and her parents were also living in the county.[173]

On 11 May 1780 Butler Stonestreet "of Prince George's County" sold to his brother John for £275 his interest in Battersea plantation which had been devised to them by their grandfather Thomas Stonestreet.[174] Elisha Williams, his father-in-law, had moved to Stephens City, Virginia, in 1779 and Butler Stonestreet appears to have followed him there soon after signing this deed. He is on the Frederick County (Virginia) tax list of 1782 with three white souls and two slaves.[175]

In 1792 Butler Stonestreet and the Williams family moved from Frederick County to Bath County, Virginia, where he lived for the rest of his life. He had a license on 2 February 1797 to keep an ordinary (inn) "at the big house in the county, he having complied with the law."[176] A renewal of his license in 1799 shows that the inn was at Warm Springs in the county.[177]

On 15 October 1800 Mary Stonestreet had the gift of 350 acres of land in Warm Springs Valley in Bath County from her father, the deed noting that she had intermarried with Butler Stonestreet.[178]

---

[172]Chancery Suit M. 6686, not seen.
[173]Brumbaugh, *Maryland Records,* I, 195, 217.
[174]Prince George's County Deeds, book FI-1, page 41.
[175]Personal Tax Lists, Virginia State Library.
[176]Bath County Minutes, book 1, page 315.
[177]Ibid., page 513.
[178]Bath County Deeds, book 2, page 381.

In September 1801 a case was tried at Staunton brought by the Commonwealth of Virginia against John Davis, a merchant of Bath County. Davis was accused of a libel on Butler Stonestreet, a tavern keeper, his wife Mary, and their three daughters Eleanor, Ann and Elizabeth Stonestreet.[179] Butler Stonestreet was named a Constable in Bath County on 16 August 1804, and he and his sons were men of considerable affairs in the county.

He left a long will dated 25 June 1835 providing for his wife Phebe (who had a legacy from her former husband Richard Mayse confirmed to her), his six sons and his only surviving daughter Elizabeth Skidmore. His wife Phebe Stonestreet was to have all of the household goods and stock "which she brought to my house after I married her" as well as part of his slaves and his land at Cook's Gap in the county. It was proved at the August court of 1836.[180]

Phebe Stonestreet became a lunatic after Butlers death. On 11 February 1845 Jared Williams was appointed curator of her person and he was also to collect and preserve her assets and to provide a comfortable support for her until a further order of the court.[181] Phebe opposed the order and it was cancelled, but John Hoover was later appointed to serve in the same capacity. Phebe Stonestreet was still living on 8 June 1847 when Hoover brought an accounting of his expenses to the Bath County court.[182] She is not found in the 1850 census.

The family Bible of Butler Stonestreet was kept current long after his death and it provides a remarkable record of his children and grandchildren. On 5 March 1891 a copy of the family records therein was notarized together with a statement made by Nancy Stonestreet that she attended the funeral of Butler Stonestreet as a child in 1837 (a small error, as Butler had died in 1836). At that time the Bible was in the possession of Harper Daniels at Danville, Vermillion County, Illinois.[183]

Children:

	i.	Elinor Williams, born 27 April 1780. She married Crawford Jackson (1792-1873) on 8 May 1815 in Bath County, Virginia. They lived in Allegany County, Virginia, where she died 22 April 1833 "in her 53rd year of her age" according to her fathers Bible.
	ii.	Ann W., born 25 July 1784. She married on 22 April 1801 Jacob Kimberlin in Bath County and died 3 February 1803.
	iii.	Elizabeth Taylor, born 22 May 1786. She married Andrew Skidmore (1779-1863) and died 23 March 1841. They are buried in a family cemetery at Mooresfield, West Virginia.
43.	iv.	Elisha Williams, born 19 May 1788.
44.	v.	Thomas W., born 26 February 1790.
45.	vi.	Jared, born 22 March 1791.
46.	vii.	John Oliver, born 3 April 1793.
47.	viii.	Butler Ashford, born 13 October 1795.
48.	ix.	Richard Henry, born 17 March 1800.

---

[179]Lyman Chalkley, *Chronicles of the Scotch-Irish settlement in Virginia*, II, 25.
[180]Bath County Wills, book 4, page 317.
[181]Bath County Minutes, under the date supplied.
[182]Ibid.
[183]Copy supplied by Margielea (Stonestreet) See of Cumberland, Maryland.

20. THOMAS[4] STONESTREET was born in Prince George's County, Maryland, the youngest son of Edward (no. 7) and Elinor (Williams) Stonestreet. He married Polly, the daughter of Samuel and Priscilla (Reed) Nicholls on 19 December 1799.[184] The young Stonestreets were married by the Reverend Wilson Lee at the Methodist Episcopal Church in Montgomery County, Maryland.[185] Both Thomas and Polly Stonestreet are said by descendants to have died a day apart in 1822 in Loudoun County, Virginia, during a diphtheria epidemic.[186] He was a school teacher according to descendants.

Samuel Nicholls, who lived in the Upper Part of Potomac Hundred with three taxables in 1777, took the Oath of Allegiance before the Honorable Joseph Wilson on 28 February 1778. He was a patriot, and provided wheat for the use of the American military in 1780 and 1781.[187] He left a sizable estate.[188] Naomi Nicholls, his daughter, died in Montgomery County in 1814; her will remembers her sister Polly Stonestreet and her other brothers and sisters.[189] The will of Priscilla Nicholls, Senior, their mother, was recorded there on 13 July 1819.

The eventual heirs of Samuel Nicholls were recorded in Davie County, North Carolina, on 9 August 1839. Bennett Clements, A. Smith Clements, Samuel Nicholls, Cephas Nicholls, William Delesdermier, Alexander Skinner, Samuel S. Stonestreet, Richard Stonestreet, and Edmond Stonestreet joined together to appoint an attorney to sell the lands once belonging to Samuel Nicholls, deceased.[190]

Thomas Stonestreet went into business in Loudoun County, Virginia (where his brothers had settled earlier), in partnership with Joseph Kelly. Kelly was apparently a silent partner and *Thomas Stonestreet & Company* was stocked with dry goods purchased in part from a Baltimore merchant who extended credit to the amount of $1278.20.[191] The business did not prosper, and on 22 October 1801 Thomas Stonestreet made a deed of gift of one negro lad named Sam and one colt to his son Richard Williams Stonestreet in consideration "of the natural love and affections which I have and bear unto my loving son."[192] The deed

---

[184]Anne Arundel County Deeds, book JB2, pages 228-32, from which we learn that in 1770 William Reed, Senior, of Anne Arundel County, gave his son-in-law, Samuel Nichols of Fredrick County, a slave named Rachel. The deed reads, in part, "for the affection I have for my son-in-law Samuel Nichols and his wife Prissillah [sic] of Frederick County..." For this Samuel Nichols family see Joseph Howard Nichols, Junior, *The Colonial Ancestors and Twentieth Century Descendants of Samuel A. Nicolls (1787-1866) of Howard County, Maryland* (Bowie, Heritage Books, 1996), 52-3.

[185]Brumbaugh, *Maryland Records*, II, 516.

[186]This hearsay account is refuted (as to year) by List A of the Personal Tax List of Loudoun County for 1824 at the Virginia State Library. Thomas Stonestreet was still taxed in this year, but presumably they did die a little later in the decade as they were not enumerated in the 1830 census.

[187]Henry C. Peden, Jr., *Revolutionary Patriots of Montgomery County, Maryland 1776-1783*, (Westminster, Maryland, 1996) 242-3.

[188]He had died before May 1807. His five heirs John and Priscilla Swink, Thomas Stonestreet, Cephas Nicholls, Amos Skinner, and Samuel Nicholls, Junior, had £55 15sh 9d each at a final settlement.

[189]*Abstracts of Wills, Montgomery County, Maryland, 1776-1825*, edited by Mary Gordon Malloy and others, page 98.

[190]Davie County, North Carolina, Wills, book 1, page 223.

[191]*The Papers of Henry Clay*, edited by James F. Hopkins, volume 1, pages 380-1, 394-5.

[192]Loudoun County Deeds, book 2B, page 124.

transferring this property to his infant son was no doubt designed to protect it from his creditors. On 4 October 1808 William Taylor engaged Henry Clay to try to recover the money due him from Joseph Kelly who had moved to Kentucky. Kelly wrote to Clay that the sheriff of Loudoun County was trying to shift the responsibility to him "by indulgence to Stonestreet." Nothing more has been learned of the matter.

On 7 August 1810 Thomas and Polly Stonestreet of Loudoun County conveyed for $200 their "right, title, and interest" in several tracts of land of land in Montgomery County, Maryland, to her mother Priscilla Nicholls of that County.[193] This was obviously a part of the settling of the estate of Samuel Nicholls, her father. Thomas Stonestreet and his brother Basil were enumerated in Loudoun County in the 1810 census.[194]

There is no probate on record for Thomas Stonestreet in Loudoun County. His grandson, Dr. Edward E. Stonestreet, wrote that his grandfather owned a plantation in Loudoun County and "being well to do gave his sons liberal educations." Dr. Stonestreet also remembered that one of his grandfather's brothers (this would be John Stonestreet, no.16) went to Kentucky where he owned a farm adjoining Henry Clay.

Children:

49.	i.	Richard Williams, born 1 September 1800.[195]
50.	ii.	Samuel Thomas, born 15 August 1802.
51.	iii.	James Edmund, born 29 August 1806.
	iv.	Mary Elizabeth, born 10 December 1812. She died 18 September 1816 in childhood.

---

[193]Montgomery County Deeds, book P, page 6. The tracts were Wickams and Pottengers, Discovery, Piney Grove, and Addition to Discovery.

[194]Thomas Stonestreet, over 45, was the dead of a family that included his wife (aged 26-45), their three sons, and two slaves.

[195]These dates are taken from a family Bible owned by Nora R., the widow of Albert D. Stonestreet, of 640 First Street, Huntington, West Virginia, and copied on 10 June 1937.

FIFTH GENERATION

21. BENJAMIN⁵ STONESTREET is included here by courtesy only. He was an adopted son of Edward Stonestreet (no. 9). His father is unknown, but his mother seems to have been Ann McPherson who subsequently married Edward Stonestreet bringing young Benjamin with her. Benjamin Stonestreet died unmarried and was buried at Trinity Church on 19 May 1833.

His maternal aunt, Mary McPherson, left a will dated 16 October 1813 leaving her entire estate to her "beloved nephew" Benjamin Stonestreet who was also named her executor.[196]

It seems certain (for want of any other possibility) that he was the man of his name who was living alone in Wilkes County, Georgia, in the 1820 Census.[197] He apparently returned soon after to Charles County where he had a deed on 29 November 1826.[198]

He was appointed the administrator of his half-brother William Stonestreet on 8 May 1832, but was dead himself a year later, an intestate, before the estate was settled.

His death set off a series of controversies between his sister Elizabeth Turner, Alexius Lancaster (his administrator), and the trustees of the Charlotte Hall School (who were entitled to unclaimed estates of intestates without heirs). The attorney for the school claimed that Henry Turner, the husband of Elizabeth Stonestreet, had taken by force the negroes belonging to the late Benjamin Stonestreet. The Turners applied for letters of administration, but were blocked when counsel for Charlotte Hall objected. In June 1838 the school submitted a petition:

> ". . . setting forth that a certain Benjamin Stonestreet of this county has died Intestate, possessed in said County of certain personal property, without any relation within the fifth degree, that the said Benjamin Stonestreet was an illegitimate child of persons unknown and that he was never married, and died without issue . . . and that the said Estate is claimed by a certain Henry Turner & his wife and the distributees of William Stonestreet, deceased, ye petitioners state that they the President and Trustees [of Charlotte Hall School] are entitled to the said Estate . . ."[199]

The Turners and Alexius were ordered to come to court and answer the petition, but no record of their appearance has been found.

22. WILLIAM⁵ STONESTREET, the son of Edward (no. 9) and Ann (McPherson) Stonestreet, was born

---

[196]Charles County Wills, 1808-17, page 300.
[197]The 1820 census of Wilkes County, Georgia, page 176. This man was missing in Georgia in 1830.
[198]Charles County Deeds, book IB-17, page 152.
[199]Charles County Orphan's Court, April 1838.

in 1790 in Charles County, Maryland. He married Juliana, daughter of John Baptist and Rebecca (Semmes) Wathen. He died on 6 March 1832 and was buried in the churchyard of St. Mary's Catholic Church at Newport in Charles County.

William Stonestreet appears to have converted to Catholicism at the time of his marriage, as the Walthens and Semmes were prominent among the Catholic families in Charles County. He was not a very successful planter, and his posterity was held in low regard by their more aristocratic Catholic cousins at La Grange in the county.

On 25 August 1813 John Wilkerson Cooksey of Wilkes County, Georgia, was named administrator of Keron H. McPherson of Charles County. Thomas Cooksey Nalley and William Stonestreet [her nephew] were bound as securities in the sum of $2000.[200]

Rebecca Wathen (she had been widowed in 1805) sold her dower in the estate of late husband on 19 February 1817 to her son-in-law William Stonestreet.[201] Her will, dated 25 February 1826, gave to her daughter Julianna a negro woman named Henny, a feather bed and its furniture, a safe and a large kettle.

William Stonestreet sold both real and personal property to his half-brother Benjamin on 27 July 1831. Included was 23 acres part of Assington, a negro man named Cupid who was aged about 45, a negro named George about 23, another slave named Alexander aged about 23, and other property for $1500.[202]

He died intestate on 6 March 1832. The papers filed in the administration of his estate show that an unnamed minor daughter died soon after her father. The first distribution of the estate mentions $20.00 paid by Joseph M. Adams for her tuition for the year 1832. Later $10.00 was spent for making a coffin for the same daughter, and on 12 August 1834 a subsequent distribution from the assets of the estate mention $3.00 for sundries for the same (or another) deceased child. A final accounting has not been found; in April 1838 Nicholas Stonestreet was acting as attorney for his sister Elizabeth Turner and the two distributees (heirs) of William Stonestreet in their claim to the estate of Benjamin Stonestreet. [In fact William Stonestreet appears to have had three surviving children living in 1838.]

Children:

i.   Simon Bolivar, born 1828. He was living, unmarried, in Allens Fresh District, Charles County, in 1850. He died on 26 February 1856 aged 28 and is buried at St. Marys Catholic Church at Newport.

ii.   Jane Frances, born 1830. She married Dr. Thomas A. Carrico (1797-1881) on 27 January 1850, a widower, at Bryantown, Charles County. He served in the War of 1812 and died 23 April 1881 at Hughesville, Charles County. She died about 1885.

iii.   William, born 1832. He married Sarah Catherine Montgomery (1835-___) on 9 January 1855. They were living in 1880 in Charles County and left issue.

---

[200]Charles County Orphan's Court, 1812-4, page 319.
[201]Charles County Deeds, book IB-10.
[202]Ibid., book IB-19, page 374.

23. CHARLES⁵ STONESTREET was born in July 1792 in Charles County, Maryland, the son of Edward (no. 9) and Ann (McPherson) Stonestreet. He was living in 1813.

Charles Stonestreet was head of a large household in the 1810 census of Charles County which appears to have included his mother and his brothers and sisters as well as nine slaves. He would still have been a minor, and it seems remarkable (but correct) that he was named as head of the family in place of his mother.[203]

In June 1813 he was put, aged 20, under the guardianship of his Aunt Mary McPherson. She was in court and accepted the responsibility and on 18 September 1813 gave a bond of $500 with William Stonestreet and Benjamin Stonestreet as her securities. Apparently the guardianship was motivated by Charles' inheritance from another aunt, Keron McPherson, for on the same day Mary McPherson receipted to John Cooksey that she had received the share of the estate belonging to her ward from the estate.[204]

Charles Stonestreet is not found in the 1820 census unless he is the extra male aged 26-45 living with his brother William Stonestreet in Charles County.

24. BUTLER⁵ STONESTREET, the son of James Freeman (no. 11) and Ann (_____) Stonestreet, was born on 13 October 1795 in Fauquier County, Virginia. He married Lucinda (Lucy) the daughter of William and Ann (Bridwell) Collins in the same county on 10 January 1826. She was born in 1806 and was living in 1870 with her son James B. Stonestreet at Washington, Rappahannock County, Virginia, a widow.

Butler Stonestreet moved immediately after his marriage to Culpeper County, Virginia, where he, his wife, amd his two eldest children were enumerated in the 1830 census.[205]

On 4 March 1843 Butler Stonestreet mortgaged his wagonmaker's shop on Lot No. 2 in the town of Washington, his stock of timber, his tools, and his supply of wagons (both finished and unfinished) as securuty for debt.[206]

He was living in 1850 and 1860 at Washington, Rappahannock County, Virginia, a wagonmaker and wheelright.[207] He gave bonds as a Constable to the Commonwealth of Virginia on 12 January 1852, 14 August 1855, and on 14 September 1856.[208] He died there before 1870 when his widow is found in the town living with a son. No probate is on record for him.

Children:

i.   James B., born 1828. He married Georgianna _____, and died in August 1895 at Washington, Rappahannock County, Virginia, a blacksmith. The will of J. W. [sic]

---

[203]The 1810 census of Charles County, Maryland, page 342.
[204]Charles County Orphan's Court, 1812-4, pages 255, 328, 360.
[205]The 1830 census of Culpeper County, Virginia, page 141.
[206]Rappahanock County Deeds, book E, page 277.
[207]The 1850 census, page 123; the 1860 census, page 217.
[208]Rappahannock County Deeds, book I, page 72; book J, page 243; book J, page 446.

Stonestreet is dated 1 August 1895 and was probated on 9 September 1895. It left his entire estate to his wife Georgia. She died on 7 June 1921 wihout issue, and on 14 June 1921 his brother H. F. Stonestreet and his two unmarried sisters Bettie and Lucy deeded their interest in 18 acres of land in Hampton Magisterial District to their two Oden nephews. Another sister Mary Stonestreet had survived her brother James W. Stonestreet, but was dead in 1921.[209]

    ii.   Elizabeth A. (Bettie), born 1830. She was living unmarried with her brother Freeman H. Stonestreet in 1880. She died before 22 November 1923 leaving as heirs her brother H. F. Stonestreet, and two nephews John W. Oden and James L. Oden, all of Washington, Virginia.

    iii.   Catherine, born 1832. She married James C. Oden, a wagonmaker, on 18 December 1857. She was living, his widow, in 1870.

    iv.   Mary B., born 1834. She was living unmarried with her brother Freeman H. Stonestreet in 1880. She was living in 1895, but was dead in 1921.

    v.   Thomas B., born 1839. He was living unmarried in 1880 at Washington, Virginia, but had died unmarried by 1895.

    vi.   Freeman H., born 1841. He was living at Washington, Rappahannock County, Virginia, in 1880. He was unmarried but the head of a household that included his three spinster sisters.

    vii.   Lucinda (Lucy), born 1847. She was living unmarried with her brother Freeman H. Stonestreet in 1880, and as late as 1921 at Washington, Virginia.

25. GEORGE WASHINGTON[5] STONESTREET was born in Fauquier County, Virginia, the son of James Freeman (no. 11) and Ann (_____) Stonestreet. He married Elizabeth Triplet on 19 July 1827 in Frederick County, Virginia; she was born on 13 April 1810 and died 31 August 1899 and is buried in Crown Hill Cemetery in Wayne County, Indiana. George W. Stonestreet died 24 December 1845 at Centreville, Wayne County, Indiana, and is buried there in the old Centreville Cemetery.

George W. Stonestreet settled soon after his marriage in Madison County, Virginia, where he was enumerated in the 1830 census.[210] By 1840 he and his brother Thomas Stonestreet had settled at Centreville in Wayne County, Indiana.[211]

George W. Stonestreet died there in 1845, and the administration on his estate was given to Myers Seaton.[212] His widow married John W. Jennings (1827-1899) as her second husband on 11 April 1850. He served in Company A of the 66th Regiment of the Illinois Volunteer Infantry in the Civil War. They are buried in the Crown Hill Cemetery at Centreville together with several of their children.[213]

    Children:

---

[209]Rappahanock County Deeds, book 30, page 380.
[210]The 1830 census of Madison County, Virginia, page 22.
[211]The 1840 census of Wayne County, Indiana, pages 504, 595.
[212]Letter from the Clerk of the Circuit Court of Wayne County, Indiana, 14 April 1975.
[213]Beverly Yount, *Tombstone Inscriptions of Wayne County, Indiana*, II, 69.

i. Martha N., born 1830. She married Jesse R. Templeton (1810-1854) on 4 March 1849 in Wayne County, Indiana. He was a wagonmaker and she was living his widow at Boston, Wayne County, in 1865. She died on 17 February 1871 (aged 40 years, 9 months, and 3 days) and is buried in the Boston Cemetery.

ii. William, born 1833. He was a wagonmaker and died unmarried on 11 March 1881; buried in the Crown Hill Cemetery.

iii. Julia A., born 1835. She was living in 1850.

iv. George W., born 1837. He married Josie Myers (1852-1932) on 20 March 1887 in Hamilton County, Indiana. They were living in 1880 in Summit Township, Effingham County, Illinois, where he died in 1882.

v. Leonidus, born 2 August 1845. He died 17 June 1860 and is buried in the Crown Hill Cemetery.

26. THOMAS[5] STONESTREET was born 19 April 1806 in Fauquier County, Virginia, the son of James Freeman (no. 11) and Ann (_____) Stonestreet. He married Sarah Twinam or Twyman (born 22 October 1803, died 9 March 1871) in Washington Township, Muskingham County, Ohio, on 13 September 1835. She was previously the widow of Samuel Twinman [*sic*], but her family name is unknown. Thomas Stonestreet died 23 April 1878 at Centreville, Wayne County, Indiana, and he and his wife are buried in the Crown Hill Cemetery at Centreville.

According to his tombstone Thomas Stonestreet was born in Buckingham County, Virginia, but this is probably a misapprehension.[214] He is not found in the 1830 census in Virginia, but he may have lived for a time in Buckingham County before 1840 (by which date he was in Wayne County, Indiana).

In 1850 he and his wife were living at Centreville, Indiana. Thomas Stonestreet was a laborer with no children or real estate. Living in the household was an Effie *Twinam*, born about 1832, a stepdaughter. John Jennings, who had married the widow of his brother George W. Stonestreet, and his four Stonestreet stepchildren, were living close by.[215]

In 1865 he was living on the east side of Main Cross in Centreville.[216]

27. DR. HENRY[5] STONESTREET was born on 18 September 1776, in Charles County, Maryland, the eldest son of Henry (no. 12) and Mary Noble (Edelen) Stonestreet. He married Elizabeth Ann M., the daughter of Benedict Boarman. She was born in 1798 and died 19 March 1849 "in her 51st year" and is buried at St. Marys Catholic Church at Newport in Charles County. He seems to have died in or before 1840 at Bryantown in Charles County, Maryland, and is said to have been buried near his wife at St. Mary's.

Dr. Stonestreet is also said to have graduated from the Medical College of Philadelphia in the time of [Dr.

---

[214]Ibid., II, page 95.
[215]The 1850 census of Wayne County, Indiana, pages 176, 179.
[216]*Directory and Soldiers Register of Wayne County, Indiana* (1865), page 190.

Benjamin] Rush but he probably earned his M. D. at the College of Medicine of Maryland in 1811.[217] He practiced first in Prince George's County, and later at Bryantown in Charles County.

On 3 December 1819 Henry Stonestreet and Elizabeth, his wife, sold to John Francis Gardiner their interest in Boarman's Rest and several other tracts which Benedict Boarman had devised to his three daughters at his death in 1815.[218]

Dr. Stonestreet was practicing medicine at Bryantown at the time of the 1830 census, but his widow was the head of a family in 1840.[219] Her household included three slaves and her son Richard. Dr. Henry was presumably already dead by this date.

No tombstone is to be found for Dr. Henry Stonestreet at St. Marys. The monument to his wife was put up by her nephews and nieces who state that he and their only son were both buried nearby.

     Child:

    i.   Richard Henry, born about 1825. He died as a young man and is said to be buried near his mother in the churchyard at St. Marys.

28. DR. JAMES EDELEN⁵ STONESTREET was born about 1778 in Charles County, Maryland, the son of Henry (no. 12) and Mary Noble (Edelen) Stonestreet. He died unmarried.

His medical education was no doubt identical to that had by his elder brother Henry. In 1801 Dr. James Stonestreet was practicing "on the western shore" of Maryland.[220]

His death is noticed in the *Maryland Gazette* for 27 September 1804 where it appears that he "died Wednesday night last [19 September] at the house of Mr. Charles Waters on the north side of the Severn [River] in his 25th year." He was buried in the lovely churchyard at St. Anns Episcopal Church at Annapolis where a tombstone survives marking his burial there at the age of 25.[221]

29. JOSEPH NOBLE⁵ STONESTREET of Cornwallis' Neck was born about 1780 in Charles County, Maryland. The son of Henry (no. 12) and Mary Noble (Edelen) Stonestreet. He married his cousin Rosalie, the daughter of Edward and Eleanor (Boarman) Edelen. Joseph Noble Stonestreet had died by October 1825.

Joseph N. Stonestreet was the head of a family in Charles County in 1810, and a justice of the peace in 1816 and thereafter.[222] He served for 27 days (22 July-17 August) in 1814 in the 43rd Regiment of the

---

[217]Eugene F. Cordell, *The Medical Annals of Maryland, 1799-1899* (1903), page 585.

[218]Harry Wright Newman, *The Maryland Semmes and kindred families* (1956), page 221.

[219]The 1830 census of Charles County, Maryland, page 168; 1840 census, page 188.

[220]Eugene F. Cordell, *The Medical Annals of Maryland* (1903), page 585.

[221]*Maryland Historical and Genealogical Bulletin*, (October 1947) IV, page 61.

[222]The 1810 census of Charles County, Maryland, page 342. His household adjoined that of his father.

Charles County Militia under Captain Francis Thompson, and did a second tour of 20 days still later in the same regiment.

On 7 June 1830 Edward Edelen made a deed of gift to his Stonestreet grandchildren; James Stonestreet had a negro boy named Austin, Edward Noble Stonestreet had a negro boy named William, Eleanor Stonestreet a negro girl named Caroline, and Catherine Stonestreet had a negro girl named Ann by the generosity of their grandfather.[223] The will of Benedict Edelen dated 21 January 1832 left all his real and personal property to his wife, and after her death it was to go to the four children of his sister *Rosey* Stonestreet.[224]

At an Orphan's Court held for October 1825 it was moved by Nicholas Stonestreet that Edward Edelen be the administrator of Joseph Noble Stonestreet, deceased, and Edelen gave a bond with Charles and James Pye as his securities.[225] Edward Edelen died in 1834 (devising a part of his lands to his Stonestreet grandchildren) and Nicholas Stonestreet replaced him as administrator of his brother Joseph.

On 7 January 1840, presumably after the death of their mother, Catherine Stonestreet (age 18) and Edward Stonestreet (age 15) were made wards of Francis Neale in Charles County.

Children:

i.   James Noble, the eldest son. He was living 16 January 1834 when he is mentioned in his grandfathers will, but died young.

ii.   Catherine (Kitty), born 1821. She died unmarried at Washington, D. C. on 3 July 1848. Her will (dated 7 February 1846) left five Negroes to the children of her sister Mary E. Hoffar. They were sold a public sale on 1 February 1855.

iii. Mary Eleanor (Ellen), born 1823. She married Dr. Ancus M. Hoffar, a dentist, and was living at Washington, D. C., in 1860. Dr. Hoffar collected a great deal of information on his wife's family. He apparently hoped to claim for her some part of the estate of a William Stonestreet who sold his possessions about Richmond, Virginia, and went home to Maidstone, Kent, where he died in 1820.

iv.   Edward Noble, born 1825. He was married to Sarah A. Fenwick on 5 June 1850 by Rev. Dr. Vetromille. They were living in 1860 in Charles County.

30. COLONEL NICHOLAS[5] STONESTREET of La Grange was born on 25 September 1782 in Charles County, Maryland, the son of Henry (no. 12) and Mary Noble (Edelen) Stonestreet. He married firstly Mary Olivia, the daughter of Charles and Sarah (Edelen) Pye, and secondly on 23 October 1823 Ann Elizabeth, the daughter of Colonel Nathan and Mary (Badan) Harris of Ellenborough in St. Mary's County; she was born 25 September 1802 and died 26 October 1879 aged 76 at the home of her son-in-law, the Honorable Frederick Stone, at Charleston.[226] Colonel Stonestreet died 26 December 1838 "aged 56" and they are buried in the family cemetery at La Grange.

---

[223]Charles County Deeds, book IB-19, page 122.
[224]Newman, *Charles County Gentry,* page 165.
[225]Charles County Orphan's Court, 1824-7, page 67.
[226]For the Harris family see the *Maryland Historical Magazine* (1936), XXXI, page 333. Colonel Harris of Ellenborough was clerk of Charles County for 49 years.

Nicholas Stonestreet was a "distinguished attorney" in Charles County, a justice of the peace, and a Captain in the War of 1812. His company of the Fourth Regimental Cavalry served for 12 days in July-August 1813 and for 64 days between June and August 1814 in the War of 1812.

In June 1806 he was named the guardian of Francis, Mary Eleanor and Catherine Neale, the minor children of his sister Jane, then the widow of Joseph Neale who had died in 1804.[227] On 1 April 1821 Jane, now the widow of Henry Digges, her second husband, joined together with her brother Henry Stonestreet to sell their undivided interest in Cornwallis' Neck and 400 acres of land which had descended to them at the death of their father to their brother Nicholas for $2000.[228] On the day following in Prince George's County Henry Stonestreet sold to his brother Nicholas for $3000 all that land in several tracts that had been devised to Dr. Henry Stonestreet on the death of his uncle Richard Stonestreet. Included was "his [Richards] dwelling plantation at the time of his death."[229]

Nicholas Stonestreet now owned both Battersea in Prince George's County and Cornwallis' Neck in Charles County. He chose not to live at either plantation and on 3 September 1831 he paid $5000 for La Grange which contained 441 acres and a handsome house that had been built about 1760 by Dr. James Craik (1730-1814). Dr. Craik had been Surgeon General to the Continental Army and perhaps the best friend of George Washington (who remembered him in his will). His house had a stairway of solid walnut and each room had its own fireplace with a mantle. Massive locks secured the front and back doors at each end of the hallway. A veranda stretched the length of the back of the house, an indication of the mild climate which made it possible to spend most of the year out-of-doors.[230]

Immediately upon acquiring the house Stonestreet embarked on an ambitious building campaign. He completely rejuvenated the interior of the house, saving only the most significant details. He also changed the orientation of the house from facing west to facing east, created a new approach lane, and added an entirely new and fashionable facade.[231] His plans for creating a fine "gentleman's country seat" were cut short by his sudden early death a few days before Christmas, 1837.

Originally LaGrange had 1000 acres and included the site of the present town of LaPlata, the county seat of Charles County. It dwindled to 160 acres, and Charles H. Stonestreet was the last member of the family to live there. James Willis acquired the house and completely restored LaGrange in 1940.

Nicholas Stonestreets eldest children were Catholics. Their maternal grandmother, Sarah Pye, died in 1830 and she provided that $3736 should be divided among her Stonestreet grandchildren. The silverplate given

---

[227]Charles County Orphan's Court, 1806-8, page 488. Francis Neale was born 31 May 1798, Mary Eleanor on 1 July 1800, and Catherine on 10 September 1802.

[228]Charles County Deeds, book IB-14, page 330.

[229]Prince George's County Deeds, book AB-1, page 603.

[230]An excellent account of La Grange will be found in Katherine Scarborough's *Homes of the Cavaliers* (1930), pages 33-6. See also Effie Gwynn Bowies *Across the Years in Prince Georges County* (1975), page 192.

[231]J. Richard Rivoire, *Homeplaces: Traditional Domestic Architecture of Charles County, Maryland* (LaPlata: Southern Maryland Studies Center, 1990) 78-85. Also at the Center in the Rivoire Research Collection, 850088, is Series I: *LaGrange National Register Nomination Application*, and Series II: *LaGrange, Southern Maryland Studies Center, LaPlata*.

to their mother, now dead, was also to be divided among them. Mary Olivia, who was named for her mother, was provided with a dowry "in case she becomes a nun." His children by Ann Harris were brought up as Protestants.

Colonel Stonestreet died on 26 December 1838 at La Grange near Port Tobacco and is buried in a family graveyard there beside his second wife.

Children: (by his first wife)

i.   Reverend Charles Henry, S. J., born 21 November 1813. He attended Philip Briscoe's classical school in St. Marys County and then entered Georgetown College where he graduated in 1833. His father intended him for the law but young Charles was called to the religious life and became a novice in August of the same year. After serving as a teacher and Prefect at Georgetown he was ordained 4 July 1843. He became Vice-President of the St. John's Literary Institution at Frederick, Maryland, but returned to Georgetown where he became President on 1 August 1851. He was next called to the then vacant Provincialship, and later became President of Gonzaga College which owed its incorporation to him. He was successively Procurator to Rome, Rector of St. Aloysius' Church in Washington, and finally Spiritual Father at Holy Cross College. He celebrated his jubilee as a member of the Society of Jesus in 1883, but his health declined rapidly thereafter and he died at Holy Cross on 3 July 1885. A portrait of Reverend Stonestreet will be found in John G. Shea's *History of Georgetown College* (1891).

ii.   Mary Olivia, named for her mother. She was born before 9 October 1814 when she is remembered in the will of her uncle Captain Richard Stonestreet, but clearly died in infancy before 1818.

iii.   Mary Olivia [Sister Mary Philomena], born 21 January 1818. Her maternal grandmother Sarah Pye provided a dowry for her in 1830 in the event that she became a nun. She is first noticed in 1850 enumerated as Sr. Stonestreet, age 31, with the staff and students of the Baltimore Academy of the Visitation. This was a boarding school on the northwest corner of Park and Center Streets in the Howard Woods area of Baltimore. Sister Mary Philomena died there on 21 June 1867 aged 49 years, 5 months.[232]

iv.   Honorable Nicholas, Jr., born 1820.[233] He married Amelia Dyer ("Kit") Thompson (1833-____) of Forest Grove, who survived him and was living in 1899. He is said to have graduated about 1834 (aged 17) from Georgetown College. A lawyer and planter, he died on 15 April 1890 aged 72 at Chapel Point in Charles County and was buried at St. Ignatius' Church. He was elected to the Maryland House of Delegates on 10 November 1857.

            (by his second wife)

v.   Lieutenant Joseph Harris, born 10 December 1826. He attended Georgetown College, but is said to have graduated from Princetown University. He married first Ann Gwinnette

---

[232]She was first buried there in the underground vaults, but the bodies were later re-interred at the New Cathedral Cemetery on Old Frederick Road.

[233]He was aged 30 in the 1850 census, leading to the best report we have of his date of birth.

Harris (born 9 May 1832, died 31 December 1857 at LaGrange) on 30 June 1857 at Trinity Church in Washington, D. C., and secondly Emily Fergusson (born 7 January 1849, died 15 April 1924). He was a planter and owned Darley which burned in 1876. He was a Second Lieutenant in the First Maryland Artillery, C. S. A., during the Civil War and was with Lee at Appomattox. He spent the rest of his life on his farm at La Plata, Charles County, Maryland, where he died on 5 August 1895, leaving issue.

vi.   Maria Louisa, born 4 May 1828. She married Hon. Frederick Stone (1820-1899) on 10 June 1852. She died 16 November 1867 and is buried at La Grange. Her husband married secondly her sister Jennie Stonestreet.

vii.   Benjamin Gwinn, born 6 April 1831. He was a student at Princeton University in New Jersey in 1850. He married Mary Ellen Sellman (1831-1900) on 16 December 1856 at All Hallows' Parish in Anne Arundel County, Maryland, and was a "noted criminal lawyer of Charles County." Benjamin G. Stonestreet died on 10 December 1905 at LaPlata and is buried there in Mt. Rest Cemetery.

viii.   Virginia Jane ("Jennie"), was born in 1834. She married firstly Dr. Oscar Fergusson, M.D., and secondly the Honorable Frederick Stone (1820-1899) on 15 June 1870. He had graduated from St. John's College at Annapolis in 1839, and was a member of Congress from 1867 to 1871.[234]

31. LEWIS[5] STONESTREET, the youngest son of Henry (no. 12) and Mary Noble (Edelen) Stonestreet, was born in Charles County. He never married and died as a young man in Charles County.

Lewis Stonestreet was remembered in the will of his uncle Richard Stonestreet in 1815 and in the will of his mother in 1818. On 10 January 1818 he receipted to his brothers Joseph Noble and Nicholas Stonestreet that he had received all his part of the negroes and personal property from the estate of their father. On the same day his brother Henry gave a similar receipt, and their sister Jane Digges did the same on 19 March 1818.[235]

On 19 September 1818 Lewis Stonestreet sold to his brothers Joseph and Nicholas slaves named Betsy, Moses, Sary (and her children Will and Harriet), and Mill (and her children Dory and Mary) for $1000.[236] Betsy and Moses had been left to Lewis Stonestreet by his uncle James Edelen in his will dated 29 August 1813.

Lewis Stonestreet sold all of his one-fifth interest in Cornwallis' Neck to include the dwelling house of his father and 400 acres of land surrounding it to his brother Nicholas for $1000 on 21 August 1819.[237]

He is last noticed on 12 May 1821 when Charles A. Pye, Nicholas Stonestreet and Lewis Stonestreet were witnesses to the will of Wilford Manning. Neither of the Stonestreets were present when the will was proven on 22 September 1824.

[234]*Biographical directory of the American Congress, 1774-1971* (1971), page 1762.
[235]Charles County Orphan's Court, 1818-9, page 363.
[236]Charles County Deeds, book IB-12, page 483.
[237]Ibid., book IB-13, page 231.

Lewis Stonestreet is not found in the 1830 census. He had no land or slaves left to devise and no probate has been found for him in Charles County.

32. RICHARD⁵ STONESTREET was born in 1785 in Pittsylvania County, Virginia, the eldest son of Butler Edelen (no. 14) and Sarah (Norton) Stonestreet. He married Mary Dicken (1790-1862) on 10 May 1812 in Warren County, Georgia. He died in 1869 at Kosciusko in Attala County, Mississippi, and he and his wife and most of their children are buried there in the New Hope Cemetery.

Richard Stonestreet had settled before his marriage at Warrenton, Georgia, and stayed there until shortly before 1850 when he moved to Kosciusko, Mississippi. He was a planter at both places.

In 1834 his four youngest children attended school in Warren County, Georgia, while Henry Stonestreet, age 15, was then enrolled in Morgan Academy.

Children:

i. James Dallas, born 1814. He married firstly Sarah Ann Ellington, and secondly Sophronie Meggs. He was a farmer at Kosciusko where he died in 1881.
ii. Sarah, born 1817. She was living unmarried in 1850.
iii. Henry Nicholas, born 1819. He was living unmarried with his parents in 1860.
iv. Butler Edelen, born 1820. He married Charlotte Jackson on 26 December 1850. They remained at Warrenton, Georgia, where he died in 1865.
v. Patience, born 1826. She was living unmarried in 1850 with her parents. She married _____ Dicken and was living, his widow, in 1870.
vi. Catherine, born 1828. She was living unmarried with her brother William Milton Stonestreet in 1880.
vii. William Milton, born 13 September 1830. He served in Company A of the 15th Regiment of Mississippi Volunteer Infantry in the Civil War. He married Leticia Ann Shelley and died 21 February 1903 at Kosciusko, Mississippi, and is buried in the Shelley family cemetery.
viii. John W., born 1834. He died in 1849 and is buried in New Hope Cemetery near his parents.
ix. Robert F., born 1836. He also died in 1849 and is buried near his parents in New Hope Cemetery.

33. HENRY⁵ STONESTREET was born on 12 October 1789, the son of Butler Edelen (no. 14) and Sarah (Norton) Stonestreet. He married Rebecca, the daughter of Isaac and Lucretia (Jones) Enochs, on 18 January 1814 in Jefferson County, Kentucky. She was born on 30 January 1792 in North Carolina.[238] They were living in 1860 in Harrods Creek District, Jefferson County, Kentucky.

He moved with his father to Kentucky before 1814 from North Carolina. He remained in Jefferson County,

---

[238]Isaac Enochs was enumerated in 1790 and 1800 in Salisbury District, Rowan County, North Carolina.

near Louisville, when the rest of his family moved to Oldham County, Kentucky.

Children:

i.   Mary Ann, born 16 November 1814. She married Henry Ring on 13 April 1835 in Jefferson County, Kentucky, and removed with him to Linton Township, Vigo County, Indiana. She died there on 4 June 1853 and is buried in the Ring Cemetery on State Route 246.

ii.   Eliza Jane, born 30 May 1816. She was living in 1860 with her parents, unmarried.

iii.   Lucinda, born 4 February 1818. No further record.

iv.   Sarah, born 11 January 1820. She married Pendleton Wilhoit (1820-1903) on 15 June 1840 in Jefferson County, Kentucky. They were living in 1850 in Linton Township, Vigo County, Indiana. She died 9 August 1894 in Kansas Township, Edgar County, Illinois, and is buried there in Pleasant Hill Cemetery.

v.   Nicholas Henry, born 27 January 1822. He married Mary Elizabeth Broyles on 9 February 1843 and was living in 1880 in Harrods Creek Precinct of Jefferson County, Kentucky, a laborer.

vi.   Elizabeth J., born 25 August 1842. She was living at home in 1860.

34. BUTLER[5] STONESTREET was born on 6 October 1797 in Rowan County, North Carolina, the son of Butler Edelen (no. 14) and Sarah (Norton) Stonestreet. He married firstly on 4 January 1825 in Jefferson County, Kentucky, Ruth, a daughter of Robert and Abby (Miller) Wooden. She was born on 27 June 1803, died 24 June 1853. He married secondly Mrs. Permelia Basey, the widow of Elijah Basey. She was born on 22 January 1806 and died 11 November 1881. He died on 12 January 1879 in Oldham County, Kentucky, and he and his first wife are buried in the Stonestreet Cemetery on State Route 146. His second wife is buried in the Barnhill Cemetery in Oldham County.

Butler Stonestreet moved to Kentucky with his parents as a child. Tax records (and his will) show that he was a prosperous farmer. In the 1870 census of Brownsboro Precinct of Oldham County he is shown as having $18,000 in real estate and $3,000 in personal property.[239]

He left a long will in Oldham County dated 9 February 1878. He remembers his widow (not the mother of his children) and set up guardianships for the six children of his deceased sons James A. and Butler E. Stonestreet. His daughters Isabel Cassady and Jane Wilhoit had also died before their father. Some of his sons and sons-in-law had borrowed money from Butler Stonestreet and there are bequests in various sums to equalize the legacies to his children and grandchildren. His will was recorded 20 January 1879.[240]

Children: (by his first wife)

i.   Isabel, born 12 February 1826. She married on 29 August 1843 to Weston Thomas Cassady (1821-1899) in Carroll County, Kentucky. She died on 3 April 1861 and was buried at Mt. Tabor Methodist Cemetery at Centerfield, Kentucky.

---

[239]The 1870 census of Oldham County, Kentucky, page 27.

[240]Oldham County Wills, book 6, page 325.

ii.   Sarah Frances, born 17 October 1827.
iii.   Jane Elizabeth, born 4 February 1829. She married Jesse Y. Wilhoit on 24 November 1845. She died July 1856.
iv.   Robert Henry, born 13 November 1831. He married firstly 16 December 1852 Ann Eliza Smith (1834-1872) in Jefferson County, Kentucky, and secondly Murray (?Mary) B. Phillips on 8 December 1875. He died 15 July 1920.
v.   Butler Edelen, born 28 September 1833. He married Virginia Sibley (or Kavenaught) (1834-1926) and died in 1877 before his father leaving three children. They are buried in the Taber Cemetery.
vi.   Richard Thomas, born 27 October 1835. He was a soldier in Company E of the First Regiment of Kentucky Volunteer Cavalry (Confederate States Army) and was killed by bushwackers in Johnson County, Tennessee, on 7 March 1865. Said to be buried in Taylorsville, Tennessee.
vii.   Lucy Ann, born 30 June 1837. She married Absalom Hawley (1827-1908) on 16 May 1853 in Oldham County, Kentucky. The Hawleys are buried in Mount Taber Cemetery.
viii.   Louisa Adeline, born 10 February 1839. She married firstly William D. Cassady on 29 September 1854, and secondly David Moreland.
ix.   John Samuel, born 16 June 1840. He died young.
x.   James Andrew, born February 1845. He married Josephine Ray on 18 September 1867 at Louisville, Kentucky. She was born in 1843 and married secondly _____ Freeman and died in 1888. He served also in Company H of the Eighth Regiment of Kentucky Volunteers Cavalry in the Civil War, enlisting on 20 August 1862 with his brother Richard Stonestreet at Shelby County, Kentucky. He survived the war, but died before his father on 4 December 1872 leaving three children. He is buried in the Mt. Taber Cemetery.
xi.   Albert Callaway, born 31 August 1844. He died young.
xii.   Charles Callaway, born 5 March 1846. He married Mary Storts and survived his father; died 23 November 1885.
xiii.   Lafayette Lewis, born 26 May 1848. He died in infancy.

35. EDWARD⁵ STONESTREET was born about 1780-4, the son of Joseph (no. 15) and Alice (_____) Stonestreet. He was living in Frederick County, Virginia, as early as the 1810 census with two sons and two daughters under 10. He is there in 1820 (at Front Royal) and in 1830 (in the Eastern Division of Frederick County, Virginia). The name of his first wife (and the mother of his children) is unknown, but it may have been Martha Ann since all of her sons gave this name to their older daughters. He married as his second wife Lucretia Phillips who was previously the widow of William Watkins.²⁴¹ She was living as the widow Lucretia Watkins in Frederick County (Eastern Division) in 1830 and married Edward Stonestreet as her second husband on 24 February 1835, presumably in what is now Clarke County, Virginia. William Hummer was the bondsman at their marriage.

Neither Edward or Lucretia Stonestreet are found as the head of a family in 1840, but Walter Stonestreet, doubtless his brother, is enumerated there. Edward Stonestreet appears to have had at least five sons who survived to adulthood of whom the three youngest were living at home (together with five daughters)

---

²⁴¹William Watkins and Lucretia Phillips had been married by a bond dated 5 January 1807 in Frederick County.

1830.[242]

No probate has been found for Edward Stonestreet, and there are no deeds recorded in either Frederick or Clarke Counties for either him or his sons. The Frederick County Order Books from 1812 to 1842 are partially indexed (excepting 1820-5) but no mention has been found there to the family.

Children:

i. Joseph. Presumably a namesake of his grandfather Stonestreet, he was living in Frederick County on 12 July 1830 when he was a bondsman at the marriage of his sister Mary. He was not he head of a family in the 1830 census and no further record has been found of him.

ii. Aaron, born in 1804 in [Frederick County?], Virginia. He had moved by 1838 to Newport Township, Washington County, Ohio, where he was twice married, firstly to Narcissa Armstrong on 14 February 1838, and secondly to Barbara Ellen Newlin on 13 November 1844. He died on 19 August 1890 aged 78 in the Washington County Infirmary. Aaron owned no real property in Ohio and there was no probate on his estate in Washington County. His widow Ellen (*Alena* in the 1880 census of Marietta) disappears from view.

iii. Samuel, born 1806 in [Frederick County?], Virginia. He was living alone in 1830. He and his wife Mary Ann Watkins were married on 3 January 1833 by Reverend Stephen Whittlesey in Frederick County (which then included Clarke County), Virginia, and had removed by 1840 to Independence Township, Washington County, Ohio. They were joined soon after in Ohio by his brother Aaron, but took their family by 1850 to Salt Creek Township, Davis County, Iowa.

iv. Mary, born about 1808. She married William Harding on 12 July 1830 in Frederick County, Virginia, with Joseph Stonestreet as the bondsman. The Hardings are not found indexed in the Virginia census records.

v. Elizabeth (Betsy), born about 1812. She married Benjamin Kent on 4 January 1832 in Frederick County, Virginia, the ceremony being performed by the Reverend Stephen Whittlesey. They were living in Clarke County (formed from Frederick) in 1840, but disappear thereafter.

vi. Edward C., born about 1818. He married Matilda King on 1 November 1843 in Clarke County, Virginia, with Marion Chism as the bondsman. Edward had died before 23 September 1847 when Matilda Stonestreet married William Wilkinson as her second husband in Page County, Virginia. [William Deahl was the bondsman.]

vii. Benjamin, born 1820. He married Roxy Ann Fowler on 13 February 1845 in Clarke County, Virginia. William A. Cooper was the bondsman. They were living in 1850 in Clarke County, Virginia, and in 1860 in German Township, Fulton County, Ohio. They later homesteaded at Wellington, Sumner County, Kansas.

viii. John, born about 1826. He married Margaret _____ presumably in Clarke County although the bond is not on record there. They have not been found in the 1850 census in Virginia, or elsewhere.

ix. Alice Ann, born 1828. She married John Roderick (1810-) on 31 August 1840 in Clarke County, with Thomas L. Blakemore as the bondsman. [She is called *Ailsey Ann* on the

---

[242]The 1830 census of Frederick County, page 86. His son Samuel, living alone, is found on page 85.

bond.] He was a cooper and they were living in 1850 in Jefferson County, [West] Virginia.

x.   A daughter, born by 1830.

36. JOHN DENT[5] STONESTREET was born in Loudoun County, Virginia, the son of John (no. 16) and Ann (Finley) Stonestreet. He married Betsy Pollock on 13 October 1807. He had died before February 1813 in Jessamine County, Kentucky, and his widow married Richard Waters on 17 September 1815 in Jessamine County as her second husband.

John D. Stonestreet is enumerated in the 1810 census of Jessamine County with a wife, a daughter under 10, and seven slaves.

His will is dated the 15 day of _____ (the month was overlooked when the will was copied into Will Book A in Jessamine County) 1812. He was then in a "low state of health" and left all his property (including a debt owed him by his brother James Stonestreet) to his wife Betsy and his daughter Serephila to be divided equally. His negro Ben was set free, and his brother James and John Metcalf were named as his executors. The will was proved at the February court of 1813.[243] His widow is not found in the 1820 census of Jessamine County, Kentucky.

          Child:

i.   Serephila, living 1810. No further record.

37. JAMES[5] STONESTREET was born 1 October 1787 in Loudoun County, Virginia, the son of John (no. 16) and Ann (Finley) Stonestreet. He married Lucy, the daughter of Jacob and Phebe (Morgan) Fishback on 13 January 1813. She was born on 8 November 1789 in Garrard County, Kentucky, and died 3 October 1848 in Clark County, Kentucky. James Stonestreet died in October 1878 and they are buried with several of their children in the Stonestreet Cemetery on the Combs Ferry Road (Gay Farm) near the Clark-Fayette County line.[244]

James Stonestreet was taken to Jessamine County, Kentucky, by his parents at the age of eight. He was educated for the bar in the District Clerks office and began the practice of law at Glasgow, Kentucky. After his marriage he settled in Clark County, Kentucky, on a farm near the old Salem Presbyterian Church where he became an elder. At the time of his death in 1878 he had served as an elder for 60 years, and for much of this time he had also served as clerk of the Synod of Kentucky.

He was clerk for 33 years to the House of Representatives of the Kentucky Legislature "and enjoyed the society and commanded the entire confidence and greatest respect of the statesmen of the common-wealth."[245] His appointment to this office is first noticed in the *Kentucky Gazette* of 12 December 1814;

---

[243]Jessamine County Wills, book A, page 434.

[244]Kathryn Owen, *Old Graveyards of Clark County, Kentucky* (1975), page 122.

[245]B. F. Van Meter, *Genealogies and sketches of some old families who have taken a prominent part in the development of Virginia and Kentucky,* pages 72-3.

he was continued in office according to the paper of 11 December 1815 and for many years thereafter.

James Stonestreet joined his sons for a time after his retirement in Big Cedar Township, Jackson County, Missouri, where he was living aged 72 with his son James in 1860. His other sons Jacob F. and Henry M. Stonestreet were living nearby.[246] His two eldest sons were large slaveowners in Missouri.

James Stonestreet returned to Kentucky where he was buried in his family cemetery in October 1878.

Children:

i. John, born 12 November 1813. He died 17 May 1840 and is buried in the Stonestreet Cemetery.
ii. Phebe Fishback, born 17 November 1815. She married Owen D. Winn on 12 April 1838 and died on 18 July 1840. She is buried in the Stonestreet Cemetery.
iii. Sarah Ann, born 24 October 1817. She married William T. Allen on 16 July 1841 and died 25 November 1845. She is buried in the Stonestreet Cemetery.
iv. Eleanor, born 24 February 1820. She died 19 November 1840 and is buried in the Stonestreet Cemetery.
v. Jacob Fishback, born 28 November 1822. He married Amelia Irvine McClanahan on 18 May 1846 at Richmond, Kentucky. He died on 14 March 1899 in Jackson County, Missouri.
vi. Elizabeth M., born 3 February 1824. She married Solomon Van Meter of "Duncastle" in Fayette County on 20 December 1842. She died 17 June 1847 and is buried in the Stonestreet Cemetery. He married secondly Lucy Hockaday.
vii. James, born 4 June 1827. He married Amelia Hockaday (1831-1864) on 28 October 1850 and moved to Jackson County, Missouri. He was living in 1909.
viii. Lucy, born 27 February 1830. She died unmarried in June 1846 and is buried in the Stonestreet Cemetery.
ix. Henry Martin, born 23 January 1833. He married Mary L. Sawyer on 7 May 1868. He died 21 June 1868 in Jackson County, Missouri.

38. ELISHA[5] STONESTREET was born about 1783 in Davie (then Rowan) County, North Carolina, the son of Edward (no. 17) and Margery (Weight) Stonestreet. He married Margaret West there on 13 September 1809 and died in Grundy County, Tennessee, in or after 1840. He may have had a second wife Mary, who survived him and was living in Coffee County in 1860.

On 25 August 1800 Edward Harben, Sen., of Rowan County, North Carolina, conveyed to the heirs of Edward Stonestreet, late of the same county, 178 1/2 acres of land on Mill Creek Branch next to John Johnston, Leven Ward, and Jesse Bryan. Elisha, John and Benjamin Stonestreet paid £200 for this tract which had apparently been owned jointly by their father and Harben.[247] On 9 October 1829 Elisha Stonestreet and Benjamin Stonestreet conveyed to their brother-in-law John Bailey of Lincoln County, Tennessee, 40 3/4 acres of land on the Yadkin River which had originally been held by Edward Stonestreet

---

[246]The 1860 census of Jackson County, Missouri, page 217.
[247]Rowan County Deeds, book 17, page 419.

and Edward Harben.[248] This appears to have been 2/5 of the tract, and presumably John Bailey had other deeds from the remaining heirs of Edward Stonestreet.

Elisha Stonestreet was enumerated in the 1810, 1820, and 1830 census of Rowan County. He apparently moved soon after to Tennessee for the marshal who took the 1830 census in Rowan County included a list of "those who have left the county since 1830." Elisha Stonestreet appears on that list, and we find him in 1840 in Coffee County, Tennessee, in that part which became the new county of Grundy in 1844. He appears to have been a widower in 1840 aged 70/80 with a female aged 30/40 as the only other resident in his household.[249] She may be the Mary Stonestreet, not found in 1850, who was living in 1860 in Coffee County aged 62.[250]

Elisha Stonestreet was dead in 1850 since only his son Benton C. Stonestreet is found in Grundy County in the census of that year. There was no probate on his estate. He owned land on Elk River in Grundy County which is mentioned on 29 September 1852 as then belonging to Jordan Sanders.[251]

       Child:

    i.   Benton C., born 1820. He married Susannah _____ (1826-___) about 1840 and they were living in that year in Grundy County, Tennessee.

39. JOHN R.[5] STONESTREET was born in 1785 in what is now Davie County, North Carolina, the son of Edward (no. 16) and Margery (Weight) Stonestreet. He married Elizabeth, the daughter of Harry Hardesty on 13 November 1818 in Fayette County, Kentucky. She was born 24 December 1796 near Lexington in Fayette County where her father is said to have been a wealthy farmer and distiller. John R. Stonestreet had died just previous to 12 May 1873 when his will was recorded in Owen County, Kentucky.

John Stonestreet was the bondsman for the marriage of Joseph M. Hauser and Mary Ward on 7 March 1814 in Surry County, North Carolina. He had moved by 1820 to Gratz, Owen County, Kentucky, where he is probably the *John J. S. Street* enumerated in the census of that year.[252] He was recently married in 1820 with one son (aged under 10) living in his household if our identification is correct.

On 10 June 1829 John Stonestreet of Owen County, Kentucky, appointed his trusted friend and brother John Bailey as his attorney to transact his business in North Carolina and in particular to sell all his interest in the estate of his father Edward Stonestreet.[253]

John R. Stonestreet is enumerated in every census of Owen County down through 1870 (when he is said to have been 90, an overstatement). He and his wife Elizabeth Stonestreet (aged 79) are living alone in that

---

[248]Ibid., book 30, page 862.
[249]The 1840 census of Coffee County, Tennessee, page 177.
[250]The 1860 census of Coffee County, page 92.
[251]Grundy County Deeds, Book A, page 20.
[252]The 1820 census of Owen County, Kentucky, page 101.
[253]This deed was recorded in Rowan County on 12 April 1830. Elizabeth, wife of John Stonestreet, also signs.

year.[254]

His will was dated 16 June 1859, but was not proved until 12 May 1873. It left all of his property to his wife Elizabeth; after her death his estate was to be divided among his three sons and his daughter "Patsy" Williams.[255]

Children:

    i.   James, born about 1820. He married Elizabeth _____ and was a farmer at Gratz, Owen County, Kentucky, in 1860. Had issue.

    ii.   Benjamin, born about 1824. He was a widower in 1860, and had issue.

    iii.   Moses, born 23 August 1826. He married Sally A. Schooler in 1857. He was educated in the common schools of Owen County and farmed 200 acres at Gratz.

    iv.   Martha (Patsy), born 1831. She married Robert Williams in October 1849. They were living in 1870 at Gratz Precinct, Owen County.

    v.   Elizabeth, born 1833. She died unmarried before her father.

40. BENJAMIN[5] STONESTREET was born about 1790 in what is now Davie County, North Carolina, the son of Edward (no. 17) and Margery (Weight) Stonestreet. He married Nancy Smith on 18 January 1814; she was born in 1795 the daughter, it is said, of "a stiller [Samuel Smith] of considerable means who owned Holmans Crossroads" in Davie County.[256] Benjamin Stonestreet had died before 2 April 1845 in Davie County. Nancy Stonestreet survived her husband by some 30 years and died on 27 September 1873. She is buried at Eaton Meeting House.

Benjamin Stonestreet is enumerated in the 1820 and 1830 census of Rowan County, and in 1840 in Davie County (which was formed in 1836). He was dead before 2 April 1845 when his negroes (valued at $2303) were divided among his widow and their three surviving children.[257] His lands were divided, one-third going to the widow, and the division recorded on 16 January 1846.[258]

Nancy Stonestreet and her children were active members of the Eaton Meeting house near Cana in Davie County. Wilborn and "Juddie" Stonestreet were later excluded from membership, but both Nancy and her

---

[254]The 1870 census of Gratz Precinct, Owen County, Kentucky, page 144.

[255]Some later particulars of this family will be found in William D. Ligons *The Ligon family and connections* (1947), pages 597-8; and in *Kentucky, a history of the state*, edited by W. H. Perrin and others, 7th edition (1887), 892, 911.

[256]Recollections of Mrs. Jennie L. (Coon) Robertson of Mocksville, North Carolina. Her father, George Coon, married Jane Smith on 3 May 1820 and had two daughters who married Stonestreets. Emily Catherine Coon (8 September 1829-23 November 1901) married John H. Stonestreet, and Martha Gaselda Coon (13 August 1836-20 July 1893) married Noah A. Stonestreet. [They were sons of Wilborn Stonestreet; both served in the Confederate Army enlisting in Davie County.]

[257]Davie County Deeds, book 2, page 594.

[258]Ibid., page 452.

daughter were members at the time of their deaths.[259]

Children:

i. Wilborn Cheshire, born 6 November 1813. He married firstly Sarah Ann Ijames on 8 March 1832, and secondly Elinor A. (Nelly) Sain on 17 December 1863. He was a farmer and Sheriff of Davie County 1872-4 where he died on 15 February 1877. His widow was living at there at Mocksville in the 1880 census.

ii. Temperance, born 1818. She married _____ Setzer and died 4 January 1864.

iii. Judiah (Juddie), born 1826. He married Mary A. Cochran and was living in 1880 in Bryan Township, Surry County, North Carolina.

41. BENJAMIN ASA[5] STONESTREET was born in Loudoun County, Virginia, the son of Basil (no. 18) and Elizabeth (?Smallwood) Stonestreet. He died unmarried before 28 September 1826 in Loudoun County.

He is, perhaps, the male aged 26 to 45 living with his mother Elizabeth Stonestreet in the 1820 census.

His personal property was appraised on 28 September 1826 by John J. Coleman and Richard H. Cockerill. Joseph Blincoe was the administrator of his estate. It included a silver watch, a parcel of books, a slave named Samuel Hockity, in addition to the usual plantation livestock, tools, and household goods.[260] No division among his heirs has been found.

42. AUGUSTUS[5] STONESTREET was born about 1788 in Loudoun County, Virginia, the son of Basil (no. 18) and Elizabeth (?Smallwood) Stonestreet. He married Hester _____ but curiously their marriage bond is not on record in Loudoun County where Augustus seems to have spent his entire life. He was living in 1860 at Whaleys Store in the county, aged 72.

The only instrument on record in Loudoun County is a deed of gift dated 30 October 1829 from *Gustavus* Stonestreet to his wife Hester and her children "which she has or may have by me, all and singular my interest in my Father Bazil Stonestreets estate by virtue of his last will and testament date of 18th November 1810."[261] His motive for this does not appear unless he hoped to elude his creditors by transferring his assets to his wife. It is also possible that he and Hester were separating and this was a type of divorce settlement. In support of this theory we do not find Augustus as the head of a family in 1830 and he may have been living with his widowed mother.

Nothing else is known of Hester Stonestreet. Augustus and his son Asa were enumerated in the 1850 census of Loudoun County; Augustus Stonestreet had real property worth $700.[262] In 1860 Augustus Stonestreet

---

[259]Extracts made by Mamie McCubbins from the church minutes in possession of Boise Cain of Cana, North Carolina.

[260]Loudoun County Wills, book R, page 346.

[261]Loudoun County Deeds, book 3T, page 63.

[262]The 1850 census of Loudoun County, page 314.

was living alone, a blacksmith, at Whaleys Store while Asa was a laborer living at Leesburg in Loudoun County.[263]

       Child:

    i.   Asa, born 1828. He was living in 1860. at Leesburg, Loudon County.

43. ELISHA WILLIAMS[5] STONESTREET was born 19 May 1788 the son of Butler (no. 19) and Mary (Williams) Stonestreet. He married Hannah, the daughter of Elijah and Eleanor (Westfall) Skidmore on 16 April 1816; she was born 9 September 1796 on the North Fork in Pendleton County, West Virginia, and died on 6 March 1861 in Kerr Township, Champaign County, Illinois. Elisha Williams Stonestreet died 20 September 1849 aged 60 at Blue Grass in Vermillion County, Illinois. They are buried in the Fairchild Cemetery in Blount Township.

Elisha Williams Stonestreet settled at the time of his marriage in Pendleton County, West Virginia, but moved about 1831 to adjoining Hardy County in the same state. In 1848 he took his family to Vermillion County, Illinois. He had died there before 12 January 1850 when three men of the county were sworn to appraise his estate; an inventory totalling $270 was returned to the court.

His widow and her son Adam Stonestreet were heads of adjoining families in the 1850 census of Vermillion County.[264]

After his death his widow Hannah Stonestreet returned to West Virginia to settle some business affairs there which required her personal attention. On 11 December 1851 Eleanor Skidmore made her will in Pendleton County remembering her daughter Hannah and her grandsons Elijah and James Stonestreet.

While his mother was in the south her son James bought 120 acres in Kerr Township in Champaign County, Illinois, and in 1853 he brought all of his brothers and sisters to live with him there. His mother joined them by 1860 when she appears in the census as the head of the family that included her children James, Mary, Ashford and Elizabeth Stonestreet.[265]

Champaign County was then a desolate area in which to bring up a family. According to the reminiscences of James Stonestreet their primitive house was surrounded by unimproved prairie covered with tall grass and wild flowers. Many times during the night this pioneer household was startled by the howling of wolves which sometimes made friends with the dogs and robbed the family of all the fowls which they attempted to raise. Eventually he succeeded in bringing his land to a high state of cultivation.

Elisha Williams Stonestreet is spoken of as a man of "strong character ... who was a highly educated man

---

[263]The 1860 census of Loudoun County, page 353, 757.

[264]The 1850 census of Vermillion County, Illinois, page 299.

[265]The 1860 census of Champaign County, Illinois, household no. 2124-2123. She seems to have prospered in the decade since 1850 for she now declared that she owned $1260 in land and $918 in personal property.

possessing great mental power."[266]

Hannah Stonestreet made a will dated 21 December 1860 and proved 15 March 1861 in Champaign County, Illinois.[267] She left her land to her sons James W. and Henry A. Stonestreet equally and an annuity to her unmarried daughter Mary A. Stonestreet. Her son Adam, her son Elijahs children, her daughter Hannah E. Stonestreet, her daughter Emily D. Burt, and her granddaughter Mary E. Wood were all left legacies.

Children: (all born in Pendleton County)

   i.   Elijah Skidmore, born 23 January 1817. He married Elizabeth Miller on 24 June 1841 in
         Pendleton County, West Virginia, and died there on 26 December 1856 "aged 39."
   ii.   Adam M., born 13 October 1818. He married his cousin Nancy Stonestreet (1822-1897)
         on 17 June 1842 in Bath County, Virginia, and died in Kerr township, Champaign County,
         Illinois, on 7 June 1884 "aged 65 years seven months and 24 days." His widow was living
         on 5 March 1891 in Champaign County when she deposed on 6 June 1884 that she had
         attended the funeral of her grandfather Butler Stonestreet in 1837 in Bath County. She died
         12 November 1897 in Champaign County.
   iii. Amanda, born 7 February 1821. [She is not living at home in 1850. She appears to have
         married _____ Wood and to have been dead in 1860.]
   iv.   Emily D., born 4 November 1822. She married Thomas Burt on 3 June 1851 in
         Vermillion County, Illinois.
   v.   James William, born 19 November 1824. He married Mary Ellen Keane (1852-___) on
         16 January 1868, and died in Kerr Township, Champaign County, Illinois, on 15 August
         1888.
   vi.   Mary Elinor, born 16 October 1826. She was unmarried in 1860 and kept house for her
         brother James Stonestreet. She died 6 February 1867 aged 38 and is buried in the Fairchild
         Cemetery.
   vii. Isaac J., born 3 June 1829. He died 21 June 1852 aged 23 and is buried in the Fairchild
         Cemetery.
   viii. Henry Ashford, born 30 June 1831. He married Eleanor Bilby on 22 January 1863 in
         Vermillion County, Illinois. He enlisted at Middlefork, Illinois, in Company E of the 51st
         Regiment of Illinois Infantry and died, a prisoner of war, on 10 November 1864 at Millan,
         Georgia.
   ix.   Hannah Elizabeth, born 1836. She was living with her brother James W. Stonestreet in
         1880, and was a spinster in 1894 at Penfield, Champaign County, Illinois.

44. THOMAS WILLIAMS⁵ STONESTREET was born 26 February 1790 the son of Butler (no. 19) and

---

[266]*Portrait and biographical album of Champaign County, Illinois* (Chapman Brothers,1887), page 218.
See also J. R. Stewart, *A standard history of Champaign County* (1918), page 592.

[267]For the ancestry of Hannah (Skidmore) Stonestreet see Warren Skidmore, *Thomas Skidmore (Scudamore), 1605-1684, of Westerleigh, Gloucestershire, and Fairfield, Connecticut*, 2nd Edition (1985), page 167. A revised edition is in preparation.

Mary (Williams) Stonestreet. He married firstly, Jane, the daughter of Jacob and Elizabeth (Holder) Teter on 10 January 1823 in Randolph County, West Virginia, and secondly Ruth J., a daughter of William and Nancy (Herron) Swearingen, on 6 August 1839 in Bath County, Virginia. (William Swearingen was the surety on the marriage bond.) She was born in 1815, and was living, his widow, in 1880 in Holly District, Braxton County, West Virginia. He died on 9 November 1853 in Braxton County.

Thomas Stonestreet was living in Bath County on the 350 acres which his grandfather Williams had deeded to his mother. On 10 May 1834 he, his brother Elisha of Hardy County and his sister Elizabeth Skidmore and her husband, also of Hardy County, sold their interest in the undivided 350 acres to William Bonner.[268] Later in the same year Thomas W. Stonestreet had a deed of gift from his father Butler Stonestreet of two slaves named Jerry and Thomas.[269]

Thomas Stonestreet was enumerated in Bath County in the 1840 census, but moved soon after to Holly District in Braxton County, West Virginia. His estate was appraised there on 14 January 1854. The sale bill of his personal property recorded in Braxton County shows that the widow Ruth Stonestreet purchased most of his household furniture and goods.[270] She survived him by many years and was living in 1880.

Children: (by his first wife)

i.   Nancy, born 27 October 1822. She married her cousin Adam Stonestreet (1818-1884) on 7 June 1842 in Bath County and died 12 November 1897 in Kerr Township, Champaign County, Illinois.

ii.   Mary Elizabeth, born 6 June 1824. She married Isaac Price (1826-1896) on 17 September 1846 in Barbour County, (West) Virginia. He was very badly wounded in the Civil War, and pensioned. She died on 29 June 1866 in childbirth and was buried on the Price homestead on Wolf Run in Barbour County.

iii.   Rachel, born 1826. She married Jesse Jackson on 23 January 1850 in Alleghany County, Virginia. She was living there, his widow, in 1860.

iv.   Andrew Butler, born 31 March 1828. He married Susannah Hines (1823-1903) on 21 October 1852. He served in Company B of the 19th Virginia Cavalry, and enrolled at Frankford in Greenbrier County by Colonel William L. Jackson. He was detailed as a butcher for Stonewall Jackson's army and served through the whole of the war. His wife was left at home to care for their five eldest children. He was paroled on 10 May 1865 at Charleston after giving his word of honor that he would conduct himself as a good and peaceable citizen and do nothing in opposition to the United States Government. They lived most of their lives at Cedarville (then Townsend's Mills) in Gilmer County, West Virginia, where he was an active member of the United Brethern Church at Cedarville. He died there on 15 June 1891 and they are buried in a cemetery on Little Bull Run in Braxton County.[271]

v.   Jacob Ashford, born 19 January 1830. He married Hannah J. Facemire. They were living

---

[268]Bath County Deeds, book 8, page 454.
[269]Ibid., page 307. (27 September 1834.)
[270]Braxton County Wills, pages 336-7.
[271]For this family see the *Genealogy of Andrew Butler Stonestreet* (Port Charlotte, Florida, 1992), by Bryan Walter Stonestreet and his wife Bernice Westfall Stonestreet.

	in 1880 in Paca District, Kanawha County, West Virginia. She was a sister of the husband of Caroline D. Stonestreet. He was living in 1910 with the Charles Rathill family.
vi.	Caroline D., born 25 March 1833. She married James Henry Facemire (1832-1917) on 18 August 1853. She died 29 May 1900 and they are buried in the Facemire Cemetery at Buckeye, Braxton County, West Virginia.
vii.	Charles F., born 17 July 1835. He married Margaret Melissa Green (1835-1906) on 17 March 1854. They were living in 1900 in Elk District, Kanawha County, West Virginia, with their son Millard Stonestreet.

(by his second wife)

viii.	Jane Teter, born 12 June 1840. She married Isaac Dilly on 30 March 1858 in Braxton County and was living there in 1870. Ruth Stonestreet, his mother-in-law, was living with Isaac Dilly in 1870 and 1880.
ix.	Martha Elinor, born 27 October 1841. She married Lewis Lawson Long (1840-1927), a Civil War soldier, on 27 August 1868 in Braxton County. She died about 1897 and is buried at Elizabeth Chapel on Bug Ridge in Braxton County.
x.	Samuel Henry Proctor, born 25 July 1843. He was a Union soldier in the Civil War, serving in Company I of the 3rd West Virginia Volunteer Cavalry. He was killed in action on 10 May 1864 at Lewisburg, West Virginia.
xi.	Melvina Ann Matilda, born 30 October 1846.
xii.	Jemina Fisher, born 29 October 1848.

45. JARED[5] STONESTREET was born 27 March 1791, the son of Butler (no. 19) and Mary (Williams) Stonestreet. He married Sarah, a daughter of Richard and Agnes (Killpatrick) Rider, on 7 March 1822 in Bath County.

On 4 October 1833 Jared Stonestreet and Sarah, his wife, of Lewis County, Virginia, sold to Elizabeth Skidmore and Elisha Stonestreet of Pendleton County for $200 his one-eighth interest (as one of the eight heirs of Mary Stonestreet) in the tract of land given to his mother by her father and "where Thomas Stonestreet now lives."[272]

Jared and Sarah Stonestreet returned soon after to Bath County where they were enumerated in the 1840 census.[273] He was living in 1847 but had died by the time of the 1850 census when Sarah is the head of the family in Bath County that included her son Strother and her daughter Mary.[274]

Children:

i.	Archer P. Strother, born 18 April 1827. He married his cousin Mary Ann Rider (1854-____) on 18 May 1861. They were living at Warm Springs in Bath County, where he was a shoemaker, in 1880. Strother Stonestreet living in 1894 at Mountain Grove, Bath

---

[272]Bath County Deeds, book 8, page 181.
[273]The 1840 census of Bath County, page 122.
[274]The 1850 census of Bath County, page 116.

County, Virginia.
ii. Nancy Jane born 1832. She married firstly Jacob Cleek on 27 March 1853 in Bath County, and secondly George W. Gibson on 22 November 1865 in Barbour County, West Virginia. Her first husband was killed in the Civil War and is buried at Mooresfield, West Virginia. Nancy Jane Gibson living in 1894 at Huttonsville, Randolph County, West Virginia.
iii. Rebecca A., born 1835. She married John J. Thomas, a millwright and a widower, on 7 April 1861 at Healing Springs in Bath County. She died in 1873, aged 38, in Bath County.
iv. Barbara E., born 1837. She married Samuel Rucker (1834-___) on 5 March 1861. She died on 28 May 1868 in Barbour County, West Virginia, of consumption.
v.   Mary M., born 1844. She married Samuel Rucker (the widower of her sister Barbara Stonestreet) on 9 March 1869 in Barbour County. They were living there in Barker district in 1880. Mary Rucker was living in 1894 at Belington, Barbour County.

46. JOHN OLIVER[5] STONESTREET was born 3 April 1793 in Bath County, Virginia, the son of Butler (no. 19) and Mary (Williams) Stonestreet. He married Elizabeth, the daughter of David and Mary (Halterman) Ross on 4 December 1821 in Shenandoah County, Virginia. He died at Crestline in Richland County, Ohio, on 29 March 1853 aged 59 years, 11 months, and 29 days. He is buried in the Blooming Grove Cemetery.

On 22 September 1832 John O. Stonestreet sold his one-eighth interest in the land given to his mother by her father to his brother Elisha and his brother-in-law Andrew Skidmore for $200.[275] He had a deed of gift from his father on 27 September 1834 of a slave named Robert.[276]

John Oliver Stonestreet had moved to Ohio by 27 December 1836 when he returned a deed to Bath County.[277] He and his wife Elizabeth were enumerated in Sandusky Township of Richland County in the 1850 census. He and his wife were childless, but his two nieces Jemima and Margaret Stonestreet were living in the household.[278]

John Stonestreet had made a will in Richland County on 2 September 1839. He was recently dead on 18 August 1853 when this will was produced and proved at court although one of the witnesses had since died and another had removed to Crawford County, Ohio. It gave all of his land in Ohio to his wife, but his one-seventh interest in the land called the "Healing Spring Place" owned by his parents in Bath County was left to his nieces Litha Stonestreet and Jemina Ross Stonestreet.[279] At the vendue sale the widow bought most of the personal property. Two turkeys brought 50 cents. The final settlement shows that $8 was spent on his coffin.

His widow was living at Crestline in 1860. She had removed by 1867 to DeKalb County, Indiana, and by 1874 to adjoining Noble County where she made her home with her nephew David Ross Stonestreet (a son of her sister Jemina, wife of Butler Ashford Stonestreet).

[275]Bath County Deeds, book 8, page 120.
[276]Ibid., book 8, page 308.
[277]Ibid., book 8, page 514.
[278]The 1850 census of Richland County, Ohio, page 778.
[279]Richland County Wills, book 1, page 439.

47. BUTLER ASHFORD⁵ STONESTREET was born on 13 October 1795 in Bath County, Virginia, the son of Butler and Mary (Williams) Stonestreet. He married firstly Jemina, the daughter of David and Mary (Halterman) Ross on 25 February 1823 in Shenandoah County, Virginia; she was a sister of the wife of his brother John Oliver Stonestreet. He married secondly Ruth H. Fisher on 13 May 1834 in Richland County, Ohio, who died before him. He died, a widower, in May 1866.

Ashford Stonestreet (as he was usually known) had moved to Springfield Township, Richland County, Ohio, in 1829 just before the time of the 1830 census.[280]

He named his brother Richard Henry Stonestreet as his attorney to sell his one-eighth interest in the land they had inherited from their mother, and on 13 September 1832 Richard H. Stonestreet sold his interest and that of his brother Ashford, now *one-fourth* of the undivided tract, to William Bonner.[281] In 1834 Ashford Stonestreet entered 80 acres in the SW quarter of Section 36, Range 20 Township 19, in Richland County, Ohio.

The four eldest children of his first wife (*Lydia,* David, Mary and Ellison) were among the heirs of their grandfather David Ross who died in Shenandoah County, Virginia.[282]

His brother Henry had joined him in Ohio briefly by 1840; in the census of that year they are both living in Blooming Grove Township of Richland County.[283] Ashford had moved by 1850 to Corsica in Morrow County, Ohio.[284]

Ashford Stonestreet left a will dated 9 May and proved on the 29 May 1866. He left his property to be equally divided among three of his sons and three of his daughters. His daughter Litha was left $5; she was insane and was an inmate of the Ohio Lunatic Asylum at Columbus as early as 1850[285].

His son Ellison was left an interest in his estate, but if he did not return home to claim it then it was to go to brother David Ross Stonestreet.[286] His wife Ruth had presumably died before Ashford.

> Children: (by his first wife)
>
> i. Elither (Litha or Lydia), born 1824. She was living in 1866, probably in an institution.
> ii. David Ross, born 7 October 1825 in Bath County. He moved in 1849 to DeKalb County, Indiana. He owned land near Albion in Noble County, Indiana, which he later traded for 250 acres in Butler Township, DeKalb County. He married Rebecca Smith (1832-1904) on 3 August 1851 in DeKalb County, Indiana. They were living in 1874 at Cedar Creek,

---

[280]The 1830 census of Springfield Township, Richland County, Ohio, page 58.
[281]Ibid., book 8, page 306.
[282]Shenandoah County Wills, book 7, page 329.
[283]The 1840 census of Blooming Grove Township, Richland County, Ohio, page 196.
[284]The 1850 census of Lincoln Township, Morrow County, Ohio, page 20.
[285]The 1850 census of Ward 1, Columbus, Franklin County, Ohio, page 745.
[286]Morrow County Wills, book 1, page 630.

DeKalb County.[287]
iii   Mary, born 1830. She was living unmarried in 1866.
iv.   Jemima, born 1832. She was living with her uncle John Oliver Stonestreet in 1850 but died before her father and her grandfather Ross.
v.   Ellison, born 1834. He had left Ohio by 1860 and was presumed to be dead.[288] His share of his father's estate was added to that of his oldest brother David at the final distribution made to the heirs on 14 October 1867. He was apparently to hold it in trust for his brother.

        (by his second wife)

vi.   Butler Ashford, born 1835. He married Sarah Fry on 4 February 1858. They were living at Corsica, Morrow County, Ohio, in 1860.
vii.   Lydia, born 10 November 1837. She married John Fry on 12 January 1858, and moved with him to Salem Township, Shelby County, Ohio, in 1860. They settled eventually in Jackson Township in Shelby County, Ohio, on a farm of 80 acres. She was living there in 1874.
viii. Robert, born 1840. According to an article appearing in the 31 May 1888 issue of the *Morrow County Sentinel* Robert Stonestreet of the 7th Regiment of Ohio Volunteer Infantry was among those soldiers from the county who were killed or died of disease in the War of the Rebellion and who were buried in the South. [This list was apparently compiled from hearsay information and additions were solicited by the editor.]
ix.   Lovina, born 1843. She married Joseph E. Ross on 6 March 1865 in Morrow County. They were living in 1874 in Noble County, Indiana.

48. RICHARD HENRY[5] STONESTREET was born 17 March 1800 in Bath County, the son of Butler (no. 19) and Mary (Williams) Stonestreet. He married firstly Mary, a daughter of Frederick and Rachel (Peck) Hevener, on 2 April 1822 in Pendleton County, (West) Virginia, and secondly Jemima, the daughter of Henry and Barbara (Barkdoll) Rohrbaugh.[289] Jemima Stonestreet was born in 1807 and was committed on 16 November 1844 to the Eastern State Hospital at Richmond, Virginia, where she was living in 1850. Richard H. Stonestreet died at Middlefork, Champaign County, Illinois, on 17 October 1857.

On 13 September 1832 Richard H. Stonestreet sold for himself and his brother Ashford their 1/4 interest in the land of their mother in Bath County which she had as the gift of her father.[290] Butler Stonestreet, his father, gave most of his sons a slave; Richard had a negro named William on 27 September 1834.[291]

In 1840 Henry Stonestreet was enumerated in Congress Township, Richland (now Morrow) County, Ohio, with his wife and three daughters.[292]

---

[287]*History of DeKalb County, Indiana* (1885), pages 502-3.
[288]He is not found enumerated anywhere in the 1860 census.
[289]Frederick Hevener was the bondsman on 29 March 1822 at the time of his first marriage.
[290]Bath County Deeds, book 9, page 341.
[291]Ibid., book 8, page 306.
[292]The 1840 census of Richland County, Ohio, page 210.

His wife was committed on 16 November 1844 to the State Hospital at Richmond on the order of the Hardy County, (West) Virginia, court.[293] Henry Stonestreet is not found as the head of a family in 1850 and his children were widely distributed in both Ohio and Virginia. Margaret was living with her uncle John O. Stonestreet. Mary was living in the household of Edmund Buck in Lincoln Township, Morrow County. Osborn was living with William Eckler in North Bloomfield Township, Morrow County. Martha Stonestreet is not found at all, and her two brothers Martin and Aaron were living with their uncle Samuel Rohrbaugh in Hardy County. They had been returned to Hardy County from Ohio according to descendants.

Henry R. Stonestreet died in Champaign County, Illinois, and his nephew James W. Stonestreet was appointed as his administrator on 17 April 1862 almost five years after his death. According to the petition he left no wife, no real property, and a personal estate estimated at only $280. His heirs were his five children: Osborn, James, Aaron, Mary M. (intermarried with Charles Yocum), and Martha E. Stonestreet. The names of his heirs as reported by James W. Stonestreet to the court do not agree in every particular with the census and other records.

Children: (by his first wife)

i.   Mary Margaret, born 1835. She had married Charles Yocum by 1862.
ii.   Osborn, born 1839. He was a teacher at Corsica, Morrow County, Ohio, in 1860. [He is undoubtedly identical with the Corporal *Albert W.* Stonestreet, also born in 1839 in Virginia who enlisted at Blendon, Ohio, for three years in Company A, 95th Regiment of the Ohio Volunteer Infantry on 9 August 1862. He was killed in action three weeks later at Richmond, Kentucky.]

(by his second wife)

iii.   Martha E., born 1840. She married Martin E. Goldizen (1850-1940) on 31 December 1872 in Pendleton County, West Virginia.
iv.   Martin Van Buren, born 22 November 1843. [He must be, by elimination, the son called *James* in the probate file on his father.] He married Nancy Bly (1835-1897) on 27 March 1871 in Grant County, West Virginia. He was a Union soldier mustered into Company I, 7th Regiment of the West Virginia Volunteer Infantry on 3 December 1861 and was wounded at Gettysburg. They were living in 1880 in Union District, Grant County, West Virginia. He died on 6 May 1918 at 241 Ridge Avenue, Hagerstown, Maryland.
v.   Aaron, born June 1846. He is said to have been returned to Hardy County from Ohio at the age of four; he married Ruhama Hevener (1847-___) on 17 November 1870. They were living in 1880 in Union District, Grant County, West Virginia. He died in 1921 at Flintstone, Allegany County, Maryland.

49. RICHARD WILLIAMS⁵ STONESTREET was born on 1 September 1800 in Loudoun County, Virginia, the son of Thomas (no. 20) and Polly (Nicholls) Stonestreet. He married, on 12 August 1823 at

---

[293]Eastern State Hospital, Minute Book 1843-1849. Nothing else appears in the files of the hospital according to a letter from Dr. Kurt T. Schmidt dated 25 February 1974.

Middletown Evangelical Lutheran Church in Frederick County, Maryland, Eleanor, the daughter of Thomas and Nancy (Gibbs) Shortness.[294] She was born on 13 February 1804, a namesake of her aunt Nelly Shortness who had married Alexander Langley on 16 January 1798 in Loudoun County.[295] Eleanor Stonestreet was dead by 1850. Richard W. Stonestreet (who never remarried) died on 1 October 1860 on Tenmile Creek in Harrison County, (West) Virginia.

The love letter which Richard Williams Stonestreet wrote to his wife proposing marriage still survives:

"July 18th, 1823
Dear Miss Those only who have suffered them can tell the unhappy moments of hesitative uncertainty which attend the formation of a resolution to declare the sentiments of affection. I, who have felt their greatest and most acute torments could not previous to my experience have formed the remotest idea of their severity.

Everyone of those qualities in which claim my admiration increased my diffidence by showing the great risk I run in venturing perhaps before my affectionate assiduities have made the desired impression your mind to make a declaration of the ardent passion I have long since felt for you. My connections are so well known to you that I need not say anything of them.

If I am disappointed of the plea I hope to hold in your affection, I hope this step will not draw on me the risk of losing the friendship of yourself and family, which I value highly, that a object less ardently desired or really estimable, could not induce me to take a step by which it should be in any manner hazarded. You have judgement enough, both of your own good qualities and the characters of those with whom you converse, to make a proper estimate of my sincerity on this occassion. I am above deceit and have not, therefore at period of our acquaintance pretended to be a man of greater property than I am, which conduces [a few words lost in a fold] and to convince you of my general sincerity.

Richard Williams Stonestreet

To Miss Eleanor Shortness"[296]

Miss Shortness accepted his proposal and they were married a few weeks later on 12 August 1823.[297] Nine

---

[294]Betsy Ann ("Nancy") Gibbs was born on 1 June 1774, the daughter of Charles Gibbs (1742-1787) of Prince George's County, Maryland. His widow Jane married secondly John Anderson on Christmas Day 1787, and they moved to Loudoun County taking his young stepdaughter with them.

[295]John Shortness (*alias* Shortnys), the father of Nelly and Thomas Shortness, first appears in Lodoun County in 1769 on a list of tithables taken by George West for Shelburne Parish. He appears to have died soon after their birth, without the benefit of probate. There may have been guardianships for his minor children entered in the Loudoun County Order Books, not checked.

[296]The original of this letter was formerly in the possession of the author's aunt, Mrs. Gordon Griffith, who died at Warren, Michigan, in 1987.

[297]The following Bible record of the children of Thomas and Nancy (Gibbs) Shortness has descended to the author:

children were born to them.

Richard Williams is said to have been a school teacher in Loudoun County (as his father had been before him).

In 1849 after the death of his wife he and his brother James Edmund Stonestreet moved to Ten Mile District, Harrison County, West Virginia. Richard W. Stonestreet purchased a farm of 138 acres on Ten Mile Creek near the town of Wolf Summit from Augustine J. Smith on 25 January 1850 paying for it partly in cash and partly in notes.[298] He is called a farmer in the 1850 census.

He died there in 1860. His will is dated 3 December 1859 and remembered his youngest children most generously. His eldest son John Wesley Stonestreet and his older daughters had apparently been provided for earlier and they are left only a dollar each. His unmarried daughter Josephine was left a third of his estate, and his five youngest sons were left the remaining two thirds to be divided equally among them. His home was to be leased out until the youngest son became of age, and then was to be divided at that time. An inventory of the estate was taken on 17 November 1860.[299]

Children: (all born in Loudoun County)

i. John Wesley, born 1824. He married Elizabeth Dilly (1829-1913) on 28 May 1848 in Prince William County, Virginia, and was living in 1850 in Turners District, Fauquier County, Virginia. He was a wagonmaker and enlisted in Company H of the 4th West Virginia Cavalry in the Civil War on 13 July 1863. They lived after the war at Columbus, Franklin County, Ohio. He was living at the National Military Home at Dayton, Ohio, in 1890 and presumably died there on 7 May 1898. His widow continued to live at 1088 McAllister Street, Columbus, after his death and died 15 February 1913.

ii. Mary Nicholls (Polly), born 1826. She married William Thomas Connor on 26 December 1851 in Harrison County. She seems to have died before her father.

iii. Eleanor, born 1828. She married John Thomas Hawes on 20 August 1847 in Frederick

---

"John Shortness was bornd the 11th day of November, 1799.

Elizabeth Ann Shortness was born the 19th day of November, 1801.

Eleanor Shortness was born the 13th day of February, 1804. [She married Richard Williams Stonestreet, noticed above.]

Charles G. Shortness was born the 29th day of June, 1806. [He married Ann Slack on 21 February 1827 in Frederick County.]

William H. Shortness was born the 9th of July, 1809.

Thomas L. Shortness was born the 16th day of February, 1812. [Thomas Harrison Shortness and his brother Charles were living in 1850 in Mary Ann Township, Licking County, Ohio. They left posterity in Illinois.]

Philo Shortness was born the 16th day of April, 1814. [He married Mary Ann Sneed on 21 July 1837 in Baltimore.]

Tamzen Shortness was bornd the 22nd day of September, 1816." [She married David Orrison on 21 July 1834 in Frederick County.]

[298]Harrison County Deeds, book 36, page 147.
[299]Harrison County Wills, book 6, page 223.

	County, Maryland, and was living in 1894 in either Washington, D. C., or Alexandria, Virginia.
iv.	Josephine, born 17 January 1830. She made her home with her brothers Samuel and Charles Edward Stonestreet and never married. She was living in 1894 at Canfield, Braxton County, West Virginia.
v.	Richard, born 1832. He enlisted in Company E of the 3rd Regiment of West Virginia Cavalry on 3 March 1864 and died of wounds received in action at Martinsburg, West Virginia, on 26 July 1864. (His brother William had enlisted earlier in earlier in the same company.)
vi.	Samuel, born 1835. He married Frances Columbia Powell (1842-1905) on 15 January 1863 in Harrison County. They moved after 1880 to Canfield, Braxton County, West Virginia, where he died in April 1895.[300]
vii.	Thomas, born 1839. He was a private in Company K, 12th Ohio Volunteer Infantry and was killed at the battle of South Mountain in Maryland on 14 September 1862. He is buried in the National Cemetery at Antietam, Maryland. Samuel Stone was appointed his administrator on 14 September 1868 in Harrison County.
viii.	William, born 12 March 1842. He enlisted in Company E of the 3rd Regiment of West Virginia Cavalry on 15 September 1862 and was captured by the enemy on 22 January 1863 at Elk Mountain in Pocahontas County, West Virginia.[301] After his illness he was paroled and returned to his company. He was joined later by older his brother Richard who had enlisted in the same company after his brother William was captured. William was discharged 30 June 1865 after a long stay in the hospital. He married Catherine Eib (1841-1928) on 21 June 1866 in Harrison County. He died 26 November 1907 at Harrisville, Ritchie County, West Virginia, where he kept a hotel. They are buried there in the IOOF Cemetery.
ix.	Charles Edward, born 17 March 1844. He married Julia Ann Knight (1851-1897) on 15 February 1868 in Harrison County. He was the County Surveyor there in 1889 (and thereafter), and a civil engineer at West Milford in 1894. He was teaching school in 1905 at St. Elmo, Alexandria County, Virginia. An early genealogist, he was a friend of Dr.

---

[300]The Braxton County *Democrat* may very well have had an obituary. Unfortunately the third week of April appears to have been lost before the paper was microfilmed.

[301]His autobiographical account of his life as a Confederate prisoner is worth noticing here. According to his pension application, after his capture he was "confined in Libby Prison, at Richmond, Virginia, for some days, and then in Castle Thunder, same city, where I occupied a dungeon every night in which the mud was at least two inches deep in places, and the walls damp and slimy, with nothing to sit or lie down on, and had to sleep squatted down on the floor leaning against the damp walls. While in Thunder Castle, I caught a severe cold resulting in pneumonia, severly affecting my right lung, and from which trouble I never recovered. I was removed from Castle Thunder to the State Line Prison, and while there had a severe attack of pneumonia fever from which I was unconscious for several days, and which nearly cost me my life. After suffering from sickness and starvation I was paroled on April 12, 1863, and sent to City Point, Virginia, and from there to the hospital at Annapolis, Maryland, where I remained one month. On arriving at the hospital I weighed fifty pounds, and during the month that I remained at the hospital my weight increased to seventy five pounds. I was sent from there to Convalescent Camp at Columbus, Ohio, to await exchange, and was exchanged in June, 1863, and joined my regiment in the field." The original application is in the National Archives.

Ancus M. Hoffar of Washington, D.C., who he sent an account of his branch of the Stonestreet family. He had a copy of the Stonestreet coat of arms and a pedigree of the Stonestreet family of Hertmonceaux, Sussex (very possibly from Dr. Hoffar in return) which he gave to a number of his kinsman. His wife is buried in the Coplin Cemetery in Harrison County.

50. SAMUEL THOMAS⁵ STONESTREET was born 15 August 1802 in Loudoun County, Virginia, the son of Thomas (no. 20) and Polly (Nicholls) Stonestreet. He married Adelaide Josephine Ambler Hall, the daughter of Dr. Elisha J. and Catherine (Smythe) Hall, on 15 December 1829 at Greenvale, Baltimore County, Maryland; she was born 12 September 1809 and died 18 February 1899. They are both buried in the Rockville Cemetery, in Montgomery County, Maryland, together with two of their sons.

Samuel T. Stonestreet completed his education in Loudoun County. There were no railroads there at that time and he walked to Rockville, Maryland, where he arrived with only an extra suit of clothes and a dollar in cash. He applied for work to Colonel Bell, then the county clerk, who got him work copying documents for the local lawyers. Later Colonel Bell gave him a job in the clerk's office and in 1828 he was himself appointed county clerk of Montgomery County, an office he held for 25 years. He bought a lot in Rockville and built a home there in 1829-30.

He was a Whig and very active in local politics. It was largely through his efforts that George C. Washington was elected to represent the district in Congress. Mr. Washington (in appreciation) gave Samuel T. Stonestreet a highly prized cup and saucer which had belonged to his uncle President Washington. They descended to his son Dr. Edward R. Stonestreet.[302]

Samuel T. Stonestreet served for many years until his death on 4 March 1889 as steward of the Methodist Church. His wife survived until 18 February 1899 when she died at the age of 90.

Children:

i.   Dr. Edward Elisha, born 7 October 1830 at Rockville. He married Martha R. Barry (1832-1902). He was graduated from the University of Maryland Hospital in 1852, and what is now the Stonestreet Museum of 19th Century Medicine was built as his office in 1852. It stood in front of the Stonestreet home at Montgomery Avenue and Monroe Street at Rockville.[303] This unusual museum has exhibits on early medicine, and the life of a country doctor. Dr. Stonestreet practiced medicine here for over 50 years, from 1852 until his death on 9 October 1903. His office was open in the mornings and evenings, and he made house calls during the middle of the day. The building was moved in 1972 to the grounds of the Montgomery County Historical Society.[304]

ii. Thomas Wilson, born 30 April 1832 at Rockville. He married Anna Helena Dorothea

---

[302]*Portrait and biographical record of the sixth Maryland Congressional District* (1898), pages 545-6. There is an extended biography here of Dr. Stonestreet as well.

[303]This was near the present Richard Montgomery High School.

[304]For an extended biography see F. Terry Hambrecht's "Dr. Edward Elisha Stonestreet: A Nineteenth-Century Country Doctor" in *The Montgomery County Story*, vol. 30, no. 4, pages 1-12.

Treadwell (1838-1908) on 4 November 1856 at the First Methodist Episcopal Church in Baltimore. They lived at Rockville where he died 16 April 1904.[305]

51. JAMES EDMUND[5] STONESTREET was born 29 August 1806 in Loudoun County, Virginia, the son of Thomas (no. 20) and Polly (Nicholls) Stonestreet. He married Amelia, a daughter of James and Hannah (Moss) Tillet on 11 January 1830 in Loudoun County; she was born in 1808 and died on 28 June 1873 in Harrison County, Virginia. James E. Stonestreet died there two years later on 3 March 1875 and they and several of their children are buried in a Stonestreet graveyard at home.

At the time of their marriage Amelia Tillet was a ward of her uncle Samuel Moss who consented to her marriage and was a bondsman for the groom. They moved in 1849 (together with his brother Richard W. Stonestreet) to Harrison County, (West) Virginia.

He purchased over 400 acres of land on the left-hand fork of Tenmile Creek about one mile southwest of the present town of Wolf Summit. His lands were covered with very fine timber and in the year 1854 he built a dam across the Tenmile Creek and erect a sawmill of the "up and down" kind. About this time the Parkersburg branch of the Baltimore and Ohio Railroad was being built through Harrison County only a short distance from his home. He sawed large quantities of timber for use by the railroad, and when it was finished shipped even more to the eastern markets. He continued to operate the mill until his death in 1875.

His will was probated on 24 March 1875, and remembers his five surviving children. His lands were partitioned among his children by the Circuit Court at the September term, 1881, and his son Alexander succeeded to the mill and 101 acres of land. He added buhrs to grind corn and buckwheat and operated the mill until the great flood of 1888 when the dam was washed out and the building so damaged that it was not rebuilt.

Alexander Stonestreet did build a fine large stone store house near where the mill stood. The site is beautiful and the stone is a fine bluish gray quarried from the old millsite. His home was undoubtedly the finest and most costly house in Harrison County according to a local historian.[306]

Alexander Stonestreet was still active there in 1940 in his 94th year, and had helped bring in the previous years hay.

Children: (all born in Loudoun County, except the last)

i.   Mary Catherine, born 10 July 1831. She died unmarried on 13 October 1859 aged 28.
ii.   Sarah Amanda, born 13 September 1833. She died unmarried on 31 July 1910 and is buried in the Coplin Cemetery.
iii.   James Thomas, born 29 October 1836. He died young.
iv.   Samuel C., born 24 March 1839. He married Caroline V. Young (1841-1928) on 15 October 1863 at Hall's Run, Harrison County. He served in Company E of the 7th

---

[305]An account of this family will be found in Emma C. Brewster Jones' *Brewster Genealogy, 1566-1907* (1908), pages 1130-1.

[306]Harvey W. Harmer, *Old Grist Mills of Harrrison County,* n.d., pages 199-200.

Regiment of West Virginia Infantry on 15 March 1865. He died 19 May 1910 at Lynch, Harrison County, and they are buried in the Coplin Cemetery at Jarvisville.

v.   Isabelle, born 24 September 1841. She married Jacob F. Scott on 8 June 1870.

vi.   Columbus S., born 1 May 1844. He died 11 December 1859 aged 15.

vii. Alexander (Sandy), born 28 September 1846. He married Martha A. Carr (1850-1936) in 1870, and they were living in 1880 in Ten Mile District. He was living in 1940.

viii. Susan Jane, born 4 April 1849. She was living unmarried in 1875.

ix.   Diadame, born 12 November 1852 in Harrison County. She married Thornton A. Rumble (1828-1914), a widower, on 14 November 1880. She died on 25 September 1930 in Harrison County.

THE STONESTREET FAMILY IN SUSSEX, ENGLAND.

The church in Withyham was struck by lightning and totally destroyed on 16 June 1663. The earliest parish registers were lost at that time. Fortunately an almost complete run of Bishop's transcripts survive between 1606 and 1641. Only two years are missing.[307] There are abundant entries for Stonestreet to be found here: an elder Edward Stonestreet had children christened as early as 1607 and is probably the man buried on 30 April 1633. Edward Stonestreet, the younger, probably born before 1607, is first mentioned as "the younger" on 2 October 1631 and had a child christened as late as 1640. The status of the children born about 1630 is not clear; they might belong to either the elder or the younger man. The marriage of the younger Edward Stonestreet is not found at Withyham and he may be the man who married Mary Wimborne on 7 November 1626 at East Grinsted, a market town not far from Withyham.

BISHOPS TRANSCRIPTS, WITHYHAM, SUSSEX.
Extracted from copies at the Guildhall Library,
London, in 1976.

11 October 1607	John, son of Edward Stanestreete, bapt.
11 March 1609/10	William, son of Edward Stansted, bapt.
20 May 1616	Edward Stanstret & Denis Driver, married.
23 May 1617	Martin Stanstreate, bapt. [His father not given.]
2 April 1621	Nic: Stanstreet, buried.
30 May 1621	Martine Stanstreet, buried.
17 February 1621/2	Robert, son of Edward Stonstreet, bapt.
30 January 1624/5	Richard, son of Edward Stanstreete, bapt.
5 August 1627	Peter, son Edward Stanstreete, bapt.
17 December 1628	Agnes, dau. of Edward Stanstreete, bapt.
19 December 1628	Agnes, dau. of Ed: Stanstreete, buried.
24 July 1630	Thomas Stonstrete, son of Edward Stonstrete, bapt.
25 March 1630/1	Elizabeth, dau. of Edward Stonestreet, buried.
2 October 1631	Elizabeth, dau. of Edward Stanstrett, the younger, bapt.
24 April 1633	John Stonestreet, buried.
30 April 1633	Edward Stonstreet, buried.
21 September 1633	The daughter of Edward Stonstreet, unbaptized, buried.
1 March 1634/5	Edward, the son of Edward Stonestreet, bapt.
16 September 1637	[blank], the wife of Edward Stanstreete, buried.
20 June 1638	Anne, wyfe of Edward Stonstreet, buried.
17 January 1638/9	John Wandmore & Susan Stonestreet, married.

---

[307]Missing are 1619 and 1629. The ecclesiastical calendar then ran from March 25th (Lady Day) to the next March 24th.

25 February 1638/9   Edward Stonstreet & Joane Hocke, married.
21 June 1640   John: son of Edward Stonstreete, bapt.

[Missing before 1606, 1619, 1629, and after 1641. The register begins in 1663; this was checked through 1700 but no Stonestreets were found. Clearly all of the Stonestreet family had died or removed by then.]

PARISH REGISTER, EAST GRINSTED, SUSSEX.

The marriages from the register have been printed by the Sussex Record Society, in volume 24. The christenings and burials, if any, have not been seen.

22 September 1561   William Wilson & Margaret Stonstret.
7 November 1626   Edward Stanstreete & Mary Wimborne.
29 April 1633   William Stonestreet & Merlin [Malin] Fford.
27 January 1641/2   Martin Stonstreat & Kathren Pring.

STONESTREET PROBATES IN EAST SUSSEX.

These are deposited in the County Record Office at Lewes, Sussex, where they were abstracted in 1975. There is, alas, no probate for any Stonestreet residing in Withyham. Nor are they mentioned in the wills (or administrations) of anyone else of the name living elsewhere in East Sussex. The probates at the superior Prerogative Court of Canterbury at the Public Record Office in London were also checked with equally disappointing results.

Will of John Stonestreet of Burwash. Dated 11 February 1554/5. Sick in body. To be buried in the churchyard at Burwash. The sum of 3sh 4d to be given to the poor people. To each of my three children 10sh to be raised out of the profits of my house and to be delivered to them at the age of 20 years and not before. If any of my children go to my occupation then he shall have all the tools belonging to my shop, or else to remain to my wife. If my wife shall chance to marry, then young John Swane shall have the profits and governance of my *childs* [sic]. Residue of goods to Elizabeth my wife who I make my sole executrix. Stephen Goodsall, the son of Stephan Goodsall, to be overseer and to have for his labors 6sh 8d to be taken out of the first year of the childs entry. Witnesses: Thomas Dawe, John Swane the younger, Robert Allen curate. This being the last will of John Stonestreet, first I will my house and garden to Elizabeth my wife for the term of her life except she marry and if she chances to marry then I will the said home and garden to John my son. Inventory exhibited totalling £5 16sh 8d on 7 May 1555.

Will of Peter Stanstret of Newick. Dated 9 August 1558. To be buried in the churchyard at Newick. To Jone, my daughter. To John, my son. To Richard, my son. To Dorite, my daughter a "heffer of iii yeres of age." To my "ii daughters Agnes and Kathrin one cow." I will unto my son [William?] a brass pan which was my grandfathers. To my wife Isabel all goods unbequeathed my debts and legacies paid and I make her my sole executrix. John Doppe, husbandman, to be overseer. Witnesses: Anthonie _____ , clarke; John Pa-', Richard Burtynshaw, & Edward Medcoffe. Sum of inventory: £7 4sh 4d. Richard Stanstret, his son, granted administration at the vicarage of Framfelde on 8 October 1558. John Doppe, husbandman, sworn. [Note: A rather difficult hand to read. The surname of the first witness is interlined, very tiny, perhaps B____ who was undoubtedly the incumbent at the local church there. His name could doubtless be supplied from other sources.] Probate in Latin.

Will of Richard Stanstret of Newick. Dated 6 September 13 Elizabeth I (1571). Sick of body. To be buried in churchyard of Newick. To the poor 10sh on the day of my burial at the discretion of my executrix and overseer. To Joan Balde, my sister's daughter, one cow. To Sara Balde, one black cow of four years, also two keyne now in the keeping of John Adams of *Fletchinge* to be delivered to the said Joan and Sara at the feast of SS. Philip and James in the 15th year of the reign of our Sovereign Lady [Queen Elizabeth], and the said John Adams shall have the keeping of the said kyne till the time abovesaid provided always that he do keep them as well as they ought to be. I will to John Dams my best coat and hosen. I give to mother Jeffery the chest in her keeping. Item William Shoulder do the owe me 19sh 8d, of which sum I give him 4sh 8d and he shall pay the other 15sh that remaineth to my executrix. I ordain Agnes Balde, my sister, to have the residue and she is to be my sole executrix. Richard Burtenshew is to be my overseer, and for his pains 2sh. Witnesses: Roger Hall, parson of Newick; John Harman, John Wells. Probated 1

March 1572.

Administration on the goods of John Stonestreet of Lewes. Given to Elizabeth, his relict, on 4 December 1579. (Latin)

Administration on the goods of Anne Stonestreet, deceased, of Salehurst. Given on 24 June 1584 to Edward Stonestreet, a son of the deceased, who is to exhibit an inventory before the feast of St. Michael Archangel next. (Latin)

Commission to collect ("colligenda") the goods of Joseph Stonestreet, an intestate. Given on 31 March 1590 to Thomas Woodd .... Robert Watte and William Ham(m)ond (are to take an inventory?) before the feast of Domino _____. (Latin). [Note: This probate is very faded and almost illegible. The abode of Joseph is not given, but since it was granted in the peculiar of Battle it is assumed that he lived there, but no "de Bello" can be seen, however. It is just possible that Watte and Hammond were sureties, but I see no sum for their bond if this is so.]

Administration on the goods of Edward Stonestreet, deceased, late of Beckley. Given on 22 June 1596 to William Stonestreet, a son of the deceased who is sworn, and to Mary Stonestreet, his relict. Michael Snepp of Burwash and Thomas Bennett of Salehurst were bound as sureties for the said William in the amount of £60. Inventory exhibited totalling £34 10d. (Latin).

Administration of the goods of Mary Stonestreet, deceased, late of Salehurst. Given on 19 January 1601/2 to John Stonestreet, her son, and Edward Cooke is bound for the said John Stonestreet of Salehurst, butcher, with Michael Sneppe of Burwash, yeoman, in the sum of £40. Inventory, £9 4 sh 4d. (Latin). [Note: In the margin "Stonstreet vid(ua)" so Mary was a widow, a fact not appearing in the sentence.]

The will of William Stonestreet of Hailsham, mercer. Sick of body. To son William £100 at the age of 21. To son Henry £500 at the age of 21 who is to surrender a messuage in Crowhurst conveyed to me by Ansell Matly, gent., now in mortgage to me. To my now wife [unnamed] £10 to be paid within three months of my death. To Phillippa, my son Nicholas' daughter, £10 at the age of 21. To the eldest son of Nicholas living at his decease £200 but in default of issue male then to issue female, and in default then to my sons William and Henry. To William, son of my brother Henry Stonestreet, one piece of plate of the value of 40sh to be delivered within three months of my decease. To the poor of Hailsham, 20sh. To the poor of St. Annes, Lewes, 10sh. Residue to son Nicholas who is to be executor. Brother Henry Stonestreet and Abraham Bodle to be overseers, and to brother Henry 22sh to make him a ring and to Abraham Bodle 10sh for their pains. Witnesses: Henry Stonestreet, Henry Cobie. Dated 21 March 1626/7, proved 10 July 1628.

Administration of the testament of Nicholas Stonestreet, late of Hailsham, deceased. Given on 19 November 1632 to Elizabeth Stonestreet, relict and executrix of the last testament of Nicholas Stonestreet.

An inventory was exhibited to the court, £63 15sh 2d. Commission on 26 November 1632 to William Osborne, clerk, curate of Westham, to administer the oath to Elizabeth Stonestreet. (Latin)

Administration on the goods of Mary Stonestreet. 8 June 1639. Mary, deceased, late of Hailsham, given to Elizabeth Parker alias Stonestreet, now the wife of Samuel Parker, gent., and the mother of the deceased, to well and truly administer the estate, etc. Samuel Parker, gent., of Herstmonceaux, and William Flud, vintner, of Lewes, are bound as sureties for £200. An inventory is to be exhibited to the court before the feast of St. Michael next. (Latin) [Note: Elizabeth Stonestreet and Samuel Parker were married in 1634 at Buxted, Sussex.]

Renounciation of Grace Stonestreet, the relict of Henry Stonestreet, late of South Heighton, clerk, intestate and deceased. On 27 October 1640 she renounced administration in favor of William Turberville one of the creditors of the deceased and letters of administration are granted to him. (Latin) [Note: William Turbeville had married Elizabeth Hudson (the widow of William Stonestreet, a brother of Reverend Henry Stonestreet) on 25 January 1631/2.]

Administration of the goods of John Stonestreet, deceased, late of Bolney, intestate. Granted on 6 September 1653 to Richard Stonestreet, his brother, in the rectory at Warbleton. Sum of inventory, £59 4d. William [Ticenredge?] of Lin[d]field, surety. (Latin)

Noncupative will of Ellen Stonestreet of Rye. Spoken 5 April 1667, she being then sick of the sickness whereof she died, made in the presence of George Wattel of Rye, Amey the wife of John Gilbert of Rye, seaman, and Judith Hounsel of Rye, spinster. Ann Watts, granddaughter of her late husband Thomas Stonestreet, should by preference be given to one Moore of Ashford to take, keep, and bring up, and her brother William Sliton is to give Moore £20 or £30 of her estate if Moore agrees. To her servant Elizabeth Roberts, personalty. To Peter Sliton, son of her brother William, all movables in the hall of her dwelling house. To her brother William Sliton all movables in the kitchen chamber. To Elizabeth Ducke, wife of John Ducke, personalty. To Bridgett, wife of Richard Bolton of Rye, personalty. To Ellen, wife of Walter Whitewood of Rye, personalty. To Bridgett, wife of Walter Chapman, personalty. Residue to brother William Sliton. Witnessed 20 April 1667. Probate granted 15 May 16678 to William Sliton, brother of the deceased.

Will of John Stonestreet of Lewes. Dated 10 August 1668. To wife Anne. To Mary Russell, my sister. To John, son of my brother George Stonestreet, £100. To Martha, wife of my brother George Stonestreet. Lands in Hailsham. Bequest to children of his sister Mary Russell, but in default of heirs then to my kinsman William Stonestreet of London, drugster. To William Clagett of Lewes, gent., my uncle, £15. To Elizabeth Burdett of Lewes, my aunt, 20 sh. Residue to brother George Stonestreet who is named executor. Witnesses: Robert Swan, Christopher Yorkhurst. No probate shown.

Will of George Stonestreet of Lewes, gent. Dated 2 June 1669. Sick in body. To wife Martha all my manor of Hounde and Longdeane in the county of Sussex (except those lands at Chailey in the occupation of Richard Bonner, clerk). To wife Martha £30 to be paid within six months and personalty (described). Wife is now with child and if she is delivered of two children my executors shall pay to each of them £400 at the age of 21 years, and to the females at the age of 21 years or the day of their marriage if first happen. If either happen to die their share to the surviving if he be a son at 21 years or if she be a daughter at 21 years or her day of marriage. If they both be sons or if either of them be a son [involved provisions for the descent of certain copyhold lands in Hailsham lately belonging to his brother John Stonestreet, which shall of right belong or descend to his (Georges) son John Stonestreet and his heirs, but if my wife is delivered of one child only, either a son or daughter, etc.]. To brother Mr. Richard Russell, of Lewes, apothecary, £10. To sister Mary, wife of Richard Russell, £20. To John, Nathaniel, Elizabeth, Martha, & Hannah Russell, their children, £10 each. To Anne Stonestreet, widow of my brother, John, £10. To William Clagett of Lewes, my uncle, £4. To Elizabeth Burdett, widow, my aunt, 20sh. The poor of the four parishes of Lewes, £4 (20sh each). Executors: Henry Shelley of Lewes, Esq., John Spence of Lindfield, Esq., Richard Russell of Lewes, apothecary, and John Lopdell of Lewes, woollen draper, loving friends, joint executors and they are to have the guardianship and tuition of my children during their minority. Residue to be divided among his children, or if they all die without issue, then to such children of his sister Mary Russell as shall then be living. Witnesses: Thomas Shelley, John Crouch. No date of probate shown.

Administration of Anna Stonestreet, late of Lewes, intestate. Granted on 26 January 1686 to Martha Stonestreet "sorori legitime," spinster. Inventory £491 19sh 10d. Bondsmen for Martha Stonestreet, spinster, were Thomas Bromfield of Lewes, gent., and John Elphicke of Lewes, woollen draper. [Note: Can the wives of John and George Stonestreet have been sisters as well as sisters-in-law? This is what the probate would imply. Spinster was sometimes used of a married woman, but one would expect Martha to be called widow in the grant. The status of Anne is not given].

SUSSEX ASSIZES.

These are in the custody of the Public Record Office on Chancery Lane, London.

Reign of Elizabeth I

6 July 1559: William Stonestreet, constable at Robertsbridge. Trial Jury for Thomas Stonestreet. Thomas Stonestreet & Stephen Stonestreet, laborers of East Grinsted, indicted for felonious killing. Presented to a grand jury on 6 July 1559 at Horsham sessions. That on 2 May 1559 at East Grinsted Thomas and Stephen Stonestrete assaulted an unknown man with a cudgel inflicting injuries from which he died on 14 June. On 23 June 1559 Drew Barentyne, and John Shapley, Justices of the Peace, Thomas Duffield, yeoman, & Richard Haselden, husbandman, of East Grinsted entered recognizance for the appearance of Thomas Stonestrete. Thomas is found not guilty. Stephen is still at large.

5 October 1559: Thomas Stonestrete and Richard Mylles, husbandmen of East Grinstead, are discharged for the appearance of Stephen Stonestrete. Taken at Lewes Sessions the same day.

12 July 1561: Henry Stonestrete of Buckholt, yeoman, and others, indicted for the burglary of the house of John Page at Watergate and stealing a purse containing £5.

3 April 1562: John Stonestreet, a juror at Lewes Sessions.

17 July 1566: Assizes at East Grinstead: Trial jury for William Stonestrete [and many others].

26 December 1567: William Stonestrete [of Salehurst?], a juror.

James I

17 July 1615: Trial jury for William Stonestreete [and others].

17 July 1620: Trial jury for Henry Stonstreete [and others].

UNIDENTIFIED PERSONS NAMED STONESTREET.

JOHN STONESTREET. On 18 January 1669 Ralph Dawson brought his servant John Stonestreet to the Talbot County (Maryland) Court "to have judgment of this court for his time he is judged to sarve seaven yeares." Nothing more has been learned of John Stonestreet. (Book BB no. 2, page 123.)

ROBERT STONESTREET had married Margaret _____, the widow of Archibald Johnson late of Talbot County, Maryland, by 5 August 1718 when they made an accounting of his estate (Account Book 1, page 241). On 5 August 1719 Charles Walker of Talbot County, sold to Robert Stonestreet, planter, for 2000 lbs of tobacco land called "Dun's Range Addition" in Talbot County at the head of a small branch of a branch of the Wye River called Brewers Branch, containing 200 acres more or less. The witnesses were W. Clayland and Ferdinand Callaghan. (Talbot County Deeds, book 12, page 374.) On 3 October 1741 Robert Stonestreet was a surety (with Richard Berwick) for Martha, the administratrix of John Vicker's (Account Book 17, page 337). No probate has been found for this man, who seems to have died without male issue.

WILLIAM STONESTREET was a private in the Revolutionary Army in Maryland serving in a company commanded by Capt. Henry Dobson according to a roll dated 10 September 1778. He is presumably the man of his name who served briefly in the Fourth Regiment of Maryland Cavalry in the War of 1812. He can not be identified and may have been a free Negro.

INDEX TO NAMES

Jane Frances Stonestreet 70
Thomas A. 70
Carson
Simon 18
William 18
Cassady
Isabel Stonestreet 80
Louisa Adeline Stonestreet 81
Weston Thomas 80
William D. 81
Cecil
Isaac 15
Chapman
Bridgett 106
Walter 106
Ching
John 6
Thomas 6, 20
Chism
Marion 82
Clagett
William 106
Claggett
Horatio 26
Clark
Francis 5
Clarkson
Edward 12, 18
Clay
Henry 35
Cleek
Jacob 92
Nancy Jane Stonestreet 92
Clements
A. Smith 34
Bennett 34
Cobie
Henry 105
Cochran
Mary A. 87
Cockerill
Richard H. 87
Coghill
Christian _____ 7
William 7, 11
Coleman
John J. 87
Collins
Ann Bridwell 71
Charles W. 10
Lucinda 71
William 71
Combs
Elizabeth Gibbs 18
Compton
Eleanor 6, 13
John 5
Connor
Mary Nicholls Stonestreet 97
William Thomas 97
Cooke
Edward 105
Miles 1
Cooksey

John 21
John Wilkerson 70
Coon 86
Emily Catherine 86
George 86
Jane Smith 86
Martha Gaselda 86
Cooper
William A. 82
Craik
James 76
Crouch
John 107
Curtis
Michael 5
Dams
John 104
Daniels
Harper 33
Darnaby
Cornelius 30
Elinor Stonestreet 30
Davis
John 33
Thomas 2
Dawe
Thomas 104
Dawson
Ralph 109
Deahl
William 82
Delesdermier
William 34
Dever
Elizabeth Stonestreet 23
Thomas 23
Dicken
Benjamin 17
Catherine Stonestreet 17
Mary 79
Patience Stonestreet 79
Digges
Edward 15
Henry 24, 76
Jane 78
Jane Stonestreet 24, 25, 76
Dilly
Elizabeth 97
Isaac 91
Jane Teter Stonestreet 91
Dobson
Henry 109
Doppe
John 104
Dorsett
Sarah Stonestreet 32
Walter 32
Driver
Denis 102
Ducke
Elizabeth 106
John 106
Duffield
Thomas 108

79

Kimberlin
  Ann W. Stonestreet 33
  Jacob 33
King
  Alexander 20
  Anne McPherson Stonestreet 20
  Matilda 82
Knight
  Julia Ann 98
Lancaster
  Alexius 69
Langley
  Alexander 96
  Nelly Shortness 96
Lanham
  Christian Stonestreet 19
  Eleazer 19
  Elisha 19
  Mary 19
  Verlinda 12, 19
Lawson
  John 29
Lee
  Ludwell 31
  Wilson 34
Lewis
  Ann 8
  Daniel 29
  Elizabeth 8
  John 9
  Mary 8
  Richard 8
  Thomas 8, 9, 29
  William 29
Long
  Lewis Lawson 91
  Martha Elinor Stonestreet 91
Lopdell
  John 107
Low
  Henry 16
Lowe
  Ann 14
  Anne Stonestreet 12
  John Hawkins 12
Magruder
  Enoch 9
  Nathaniel 16
Manning
  Wilford 78
Marbury
  Luke 16
Markland
  Jonathan 26
Marshall
  James 9
Mason
  Philip 8, 10
  Samuel 10
Massey
  Elizabeth Tyler 9
  Henry 9
Mastin
  Robert 4

  Thomas 3, 4
Matly
  Ansell 105
Mattingly
  Elizabeth 20
  Elizabeth Stonestreet 14
Mayse
  Richard 32, 33
McClanahan
  Amelia Irvine 84
McCongh
  James 2
McConnell
  James 28
McCormick
  Joseph 6
McGinty
  James 26, 27
McPherson
  Ann 69
  Anne 20
  Charles 21
  Elinor Wilkinson 20
  Karenhappock 21
  Karren 21
  Keron 71
  Keron H. 70
  Mary 21, 69, 71
  Walter 21
  William 20
Medcoffe
  Edward 104
Meggs
  Sophronie 79
Metcalf
  John 83
Miller
  Abby 80
  Elizabeth 89
  Thomas 1
Minnick
  Phebe 32
  Simon 32
Mohoy
  James 2
Montgomery
  Sarah Catherine 70
Moreland
  David 81
  Louisa Adeline Stonestreet 81
Morris
  Richard 1
Moss
  Hannah 100
  Samuel 100
Mullican
  Lewis 26
Myers
  Josie 73
Mylles
  Richard 108
Nalley
  Thomas Cooksey 70
Neale

82

Mary 82
Rohrbaugh
  Barbara Barkdoll 94
  Henry 94
  Jemina 94
  Samuel 95
Ross
  David 92, 93
  Elizabeth 92
  Joseph E. 94
  Lovina Stonestreet 94
  Mary Halterman 92, 93
Rozier
  Benjamin 7
Rucker
  Barbara E. Stonestreet 92
  Mary M. Stonestreet 92
  Samuel 92
Rumble
  Diadame Stonestreet 101
  Thornton A. 101
Rush
  Benjamin 74
Russell
  Mary 106
  Richard 107
Sain
  Elinor A. 87
Sanders
  Jordan 85
Sawyer
  Mary L. 84
Schooler
  Sally A. 86
Scott
  Isabelle Stonestreet 101
  Jacob F. 101
See
  Margielea Stonestreet 33
Sellman
  Mary Ellen 78
Setzer
  Temperance Stonestreet 87
Shapley
  John 108
Shaw
  George 1
Shelley
  Henry 107
  Leticia Ann 79
  Thomas 107
Sheppard
  John 2
Shortness
  Charles G. 97
  Eleanor 96, 97
  Elizabeth Ann 97
  John 97
  Nancy Gibbs 96
  Nelly 96
  Philo 97
  Tamzen 97
  Thomas 96
  Thomas L. 97

William H. 97
Shoulder
  William 104
Sibley
  Virginia 81
Skidmore
  Andrew 33, 92
  Eleanor Westfall 88
  Elijah 88
  Elizabeth 33, 90, 91
  Elizabeth Taylor Stonetreet 33
  Hannah 88
Skinner
  Alexander 34
  Amos 34
Slaves
  Alexander 70
  Amy 19
  Ann 75
  Anne 19
  Anney 29
  Austin 75
  Ben 25, 29, 83
  Betsy 12, 78
  Bill 31
  Billy 31
  Bob 29
  Burrell 22
  Caroline 75
  Cate 12
  Chales 31
  Charles 12
  Cupid 70
  Dory 78
  Ed 12
  Fanny 25
  George 70
  Hannah 29
  Harry 12, 31
  Henny 15, 70
  Jack 11, 12, 19
  James 19, 31
  Jenny 29
  Jerry 19, 90
  Judah 29
  Kate 11
  Lewis 29
  Liddy 31
  Little Macy 15
  Lydia 19
  Mary 22, 78
  Massey 12
  Mill 78
  Moses 19, 27, 31, 78
  Nace 29
  Pat 29
  Patience 11, 12
  Patient 31
  Patty 31
  Pen 29
  Penny 19
  Peter 22
  Phillis 29
  Pinder 19

William 8, 9
Van Meter
    Elizabeth M. Stonestreet 84
    Lucy Hockaday 84
    Solomon 84
Vicker
    John 109
Vincent
    Moses 26
Wade
    Richard 15
    Robert 12, 18
Walker
    James 1
Walton
    John 5
Wandmore
    John 102
Ward
    Leven 84
    Mary 85
Warren
    Humphrey 3
Washington
    George 13, 17, 23, 76, 99
    George C. 99
Waters
    Betsey Pollock 83
    Charles 74
    Richard 83
    William 1
Wathen
    John Baptist 70
    Juliana 70
    Rebecca Semmes 70
Watkins
    Lucretia Phillips 81
    Mary Ann 82
    William 81
    Williams 81
Watte
    Robert 105
Wattel
    George 106
Watts
    Ann 106
Weight
    Margery 30
Wells
    John 104
West
    Margaret 84
Wheeler
    Clement 15
    Jane Edelen 15
White
    Anne Stonestreet 27
Whitewood
    Ellen 106
    Walter 106
Whittier
    George 5
Whittlesey
    Stephen 82

Wilhoit
    Jane Elizabeth Stonestreet 81
    Jesse Y. 81
    Pendleton 80
    Sarah Stonestreet 80
Wilkinson
    Matilda King 82
    William 82
William
    Stonestreet 98
Williams
    Ann Swearingen 32
    Basil 18
    Elinor 17
    Elisha 18, 32
    Jared 33
    John 18
    Martha Stonestreet 86
    Mary 32
    Mary _____ 18
    Robert 86
    Thomas 18
Willis
    James 76
Wilson
    Joseph 34
    William 103
Wimborne
    Mary 102, 103
Winn
    Owen D. 84
    Phebe Fishback Stonestreet 84
Winter
    John 20
Wood
    Amanda Stonestreet 89
    Mary E. 89
Woodd
    Thomas 105
Wooden
    Abby Miller 80
    Robert 80
    Ruth 80
Yocum
    Charles 95
    Mary Margaret Stonestreet 95
Yorkhurst
    Christopher 106
Young
    Caroline V. 100

Made in United States
Troutdale, OR
10/19/2024